Better Homes and Gardens®

COUNTRY STYLE

BETTER HOMES AND GARDENS® BOOKS
Editor: Gerald M. Knox
Art Director: Ernest Shelton
Managing Editor: David A. Kirchner

Furnishings and Design Editor: Shirley Van Zante
Senior Furnishings Editor, Books: Sharon L. Novotne O'Keefe

Copy and Production Editors: James D. Blume, Marsha Jahns,
    Rosanne Weber Mattson, Mary Helen Schiltz
Associate Art Directors: Linda Ford Vermie, Neoma Alt West, Randall Yontz
Assistant Art Directors: Lynda Haupert, Harijs Priekulis, Tom Wegner
Senior Graphic Designers: Jack Murphy, Stan Sams, Darla Whipple-Frain
Graphic Designers: Mike Burns, Sally Cooper, Blake Welch, Brian Wignall

Vice President, Editorial Director: Doris Eby
Executive Director, Editorial Services: Duane L. Gregg

President, Book Group: Fred Stines
Vice President, Retail Marketing: Jamie Martin
Vice President, Direct Marketing: Arthur Heydendael

Country Style
Editor: Sharon L. Novotne O'Keefe
Copy and Production Editor: Marsha Jahns
Graphic Designer: Tom Wegner
Electronic Text Processor: Paula Forest

Special thanks to Sandra Battin, Denise L. Caringer, Babs Klein,
Jack Parker Antiques, Rosemary Rennicke, Heather J. Schradle,
Sisler & Kovac Inc., Pamela Wilson, and Lois and Zim Zimmerman

Better Homes and Gardens® *Country Style* celebrates the matchless charm, versatility, and evolving beauty of America's premier decorating choice. From city high rises to rural retreats, in old houses and new, country is the catalyst that has focused home decorating on comfort and truly personal style. Whether you're a newcomer to country or a devotee long enchanted by its charms, let *Country Style* be your guide on a tour of beautiful homes and historic villages, each brimming with bright new ideas for today's country life-style.

Contents

The Country Home

The serenity of country life beckons from every compass point, from the venerable New England saltbox and rustic north-woods cabin to the midwestern farmstead and high-plains desert adobe. Those people who answer share a life-style philosophy highly personal and satisfying, and their homes reflect a special sense of warmth, history, and continuity. Here, five families welcome you home in eloquent country style.

The Country Home

Preserving the 'Jelly House' Legacy

Since its original owners sold orchard-fresh preserves here, the 1732 New England farm home, *left,* has been known as the "Jelly House." Today, Elizabeth and Carlton E. "Tuck" Nichols, Jr., show the fruits of their labor in a different way— through the loving renovation of their historic home. It is a mix of past and present, like the collection, *above,* of old treasures and new basketry.   *continued*

By far the most formal room in the Nicholses' Harvard, Massachusetts home, the living room, *left,* radiates the comfort and congeniality of an English-style library. To achieve this mood of easygoing elegance, they first changed the colonial color scheme, stripping old mustard-yellow paint from the ceiling beams to uncover the warmth of natural pine. Walls and woodwork were painted a deep moss green, with crisp white accent in the window trim. Deep-toned seating pieces vary in style from a traditional wing chair to the contemporary sectional sofa, draped in a paisley shawl. New light-pine paneling on the fireplace wall, *above,* was matched to existing paneling when the home's original "borning room" was annexed to create this luxurious space.

continued

What looks like a traditional patterned wall covering in the dining room, *left,* is actually a stenciled treatment. These bittersweet motifs add the desired homespun touch, but the couple knew such an intricate pattern could easily overwhelm. Thus, they balanced the vertical stenciling design with sage-green wainscoting, repeating the soft color on the corner cupboard. The cupboard's interior remains natural pine, offering a warm-hued showcase for the family's collection of silver pieces.

Continuing the theme of old meets new, Elizabeth and Tuck teamed a new vintage-style dining table and Hitchcock chairs with an antique mirror and drop-leaf side table. Even the antique Chinese porcelain, *above,* has been modernized by turning the vase into a table lamp.

continued

13

Preserving the 'Jelly House' Legacy
(continued)

Parents of two youngsters, Elizabeth and Tuck wanted a peaceful retreat away from family hustle and bustle. The master bedroom, *below,* is just that, an end-of-the-day haven, awash in soothing hues. With the majestic four-poster nearly grazing the room's low ceiling, the focus here is proportionately low. Charming accents are the flower-strewn dust ruffle, tied up in bows at the bed posts, and a bounty of ruffled and embroidered pillows that Elizabeth made from handkerchiefs.

Their young daughter's bedroom, *below,* was designed to grow in style. There's plenty of room now for toys and other childhood treasures. In a few years, the space easily can be adapted to grown-up tastes. The delicately sprigged-and-striped wallpaper will make the tot-to-teen transition beautifully.

Woodwork and trim on the "belly windows" (the right height for little ones, but waist high for adults) carry the pattern's soft green hue. Though the pine beds have vintage country appeal, they are new designs that the couple assembled from kits. Bedecked infloral comforters and white eyelet dust ruffles, the twin sleeping spots stand ready for spur-of-the-moment sleep-overs. *continued*

Preserving the 'Jelly House' Legacy
(continued)

For everyday dining, the Nichols family gathers in the sunny niche, *right.* The timeworn beams in this off-the-kitchen eating area evidence the room's past life as part of the property's barn, long ago joined to the main living quarters. The new multipaned bay window affords a view of the flagstone terrace, the couple's favorite stage for warm-weather entertaining because of its proximity to the kitchen.

Reproduction Windsor chairs accommodate diners around the rustic farm table that can be pulled away from the window for extra seating. Country French prints, in cushions and place mats, colorfully accent the seating and sill, now a showcase for collectibles set among baskets of blooming plants.

At the end of the day, the perfect place for the family to relax together and catch a breeze is the sun-dappled screened porch, *above.* Renewed with paints in romantic colors and fabrics in sprightly prints, the old seating pieces make comfort a priority and the porch an inviting retreat.

The Country Home
An Old Barn Renaissance

For more than three centuries, the Willow Farm barn sat in the long shadow of Windsor Castle, a silent witness to palace intrigue and the historic comings and goings of England's monarchs. With rough-hewn beams and cathedrallike spaces, the humble barn was, in its own way, as architecturally magnificent as its famed neighbors—the castle's great Round Tower and the hall Christopher Wren built in the Thames-side town of Windsor.

A latter-day colonist, this 17th-century antique recently arrived in America to become John and Lynn Falkowski's Bridgehampton, New York, home. Its exterior, *left,* is sheathed in new red cedar shingles, but its old oak timbers are a beautiful backdrop for country furnishings and treasures, such as those in the entry, *above.*
continued

An Old Barn Renaissance
(continued)

Enchanted by the inherent rustic character, grand spaces, and interplay of weathered beams only a barn-turned-home can offer, the couple set off on a quest through the fields of England to find the right relic. Before their barn was shipped in a puzzle of coded pieces ready for reconstruction, it was dismantled and its timbers cleaned and repaired. Then the frame was re-erected on the original site for a final inspection before it set sail.

A designer and builder expert in barn transformations, John enclosed the centuries-old frame within a new structure, adding dramatic multipaned windows, new brickwork, and expanded bedroom-and-bath space. In the living room, *right,* the new fireplace, with an old timber for its mantel, is centered in what was the barn's back door.

Beneath the imposing beams, John and Lynn chose bright colors and simple country-flavored furnishings to complement the uncommon warmth of the barn's free-flowing interior. Paired before the living room hearth, overstuffed sofas are clad in a rosy-red English print and accented with antique textiles. Old crockery jugs perched on the open timbers, primitive tools, and wicker baskets look like they, too, served a working farm where real-life counterparts of the folk-art roosters on the tabletops once roamed.

continued

An Old Barn Renaissance

(continued)

Preserving the barn's historic mien was the Falkowskis' priority, so new interior embellishments needed a timeworn look. To celebrate their barn raising and impart instant character to the new pine flooring, they hosted an "aging" party. After spilling sand and pebbles over the new floorboards, they invited the crowd to scuff up the floor before the final protective finish was added.

A barn's dominant beams and expansive spaces demand a thoughtful design approach in creating separate living areas. In the dining room, *right,* the convivial centerpiece is an antique table, 14 feet long, placed on an angle to subtly define the change of function. Each carefully selected piece of furniture, such as the scrubbed pine sideboard and the antique chairs flanking the table, takes on an objet d'art quality and seems to float within the gallerylike space. Beyond the table is an old steel-mesh wine case.

Streaming through the new French doors and windows that enclose the barn's original entry, sunlight floods the interior, casting the arcs and angles of the old timbers in dramatic shadows. On some of the beams, the original carpenter's marks—an autograph of the barn's 17th-century builder—are visible. By night, spotlighting from atop the rafters illuminates the living areas. *continued*

The historic Willow Farm barn is undeniably the heart of the Falkowskis' home, but their exacting attention to detail sets new living areas in beautiful harmony with the old. A doorway behind the living room fireplace leads to the cozy bedroom, *right,* tucked into a new addition. Although the bedroom is not part of the original barn structure, its nostalgic furnishings and newly built fireplace with barn-timber mantel match the home's pervasive warmth and character. The pine armoire is antique, but the pine four-poster is a reproduction, aptly dressed in old linens and topped with a vintage patchwork quilt.

Avid collectors who browse the antiques shops throughout New England and Long Island, John and Lynn have found, in the barn, the perfect rustic gallery for their spirited mix of treasures. In this sun-dappled corner, *above,* just inside the barn's front door, an antique spinning wheel is fittingly displayed as fine sculpture.

A Colonial Farmhouse Revival

Edged in fragrant herbs and blossoms, the stepping-stone path, *above,* guides visitors back to the future, to a 1722 Connecticut farmhouse transformed into a welcoming 1980s retreat.

The colonial-era exterior, *left,* reflects the intuitive vision of owners Ray Gaulke and Arlene Hoffman, who restored it with uncanny accuracy. After they altered the windows, an old photograph confirmed they had—unknowingly—replicated the original design. Even a new stone wall topped with weathered pickets looks as if it has *always* been there. Inside, however, the spirited furnishings are geared to today. *continued*

27

A Colonial Farmhouse Revival
(continued)

Making the most of architectural assets—rustic beams and plank floors—Arlene and Ray polished when possible and rebuilt when necessary. The music room, *right*, combines American antiques and reproduction seating for a period mood. A new wood stove adds efficiency to the old stone-faced fireplace. The dining room, *above*, best conveys the home's eclectic design. Here sleek director's-style chairs flank an old French table, and contemporary art accents the rich red walls.

continued

A Colonial Farmhouse Revival

(continued)

Radiating all the warmth of the past yet up-to-date in comfort, the living room, *right,* reflects the couple's decorating priority—to create an inviting home, not a museum. It beckons with sink-in sofas, a slick Eames lounge chair, and antique collectibles that lend traditional balance to the contemporary seating. Found in the attic, old extra-wide boards now panel the fireplace wall, *above.* Beyond the hearth, an English gateleg table and Windsor chairs are set within easy reach of volumes in the new floor-to-ceiling library. The room has a "tomahawk" front door, so named because vertical outside panels worked with horizontal inside panels to resist Indians' tomahawks.

continued

A Colonial Farmhouse Revival
(continued)

Glimpsed through the home's back door, the kitchen's massive hearth, *above,* and old smoke-darkened beams convinced the couple to buy the house. The newly crafted table, *right,* is topped with extra-wide floorboards, called King's boards, found in the attic. Since 18th-century colonists were taxed on such planks, Ray and Arlene surmise these treasures may have been hidden long ago. Whether for informal feasts at the plank table or just relaxing on the tufted sofa at fireside, this live-in kitchen captures the convivial essence and function of colonial keeping rooms.

Country Blues In Southwest Harmony

Susan and Peter Connelly's quest for a dream home led them past the picture-perfect variety to a house in need of an update. At the hands of these avid remodelers, this 1950s ranch home in Santa Fe, New Mexico, emerged in easy-living country style, from its cloistered front entry, *above,* to its sunny back deck, *left.* They raised the roof, added numerous windows, and brushed rooms in bright-white paint with soft blues in furnishings and accents, transforming the once-dark interior into a light and airy showplace for their collection of south-western antiques. *continued*

Country Blues
In Southwest Harmony
(continued)

The Connellys are masters of structural sleight of hand. To remedy the home's tunnel-like look and claustrophobic feel, Susan and Peter decided to tear out the ceiling in the 17x36-foot main living area, then raise the roof to a lofty 18-foot pitch. It was a strategy that paid off beautifully.

Whitewashed and shimmering in Santa Fe sunlight from a window bank in the dining area, *left,* and new panes flanking the fireplace, this open-plan living space makes an eye-catching statement on behalf of Southwest style. The new glazed-tile floor is one hard-working feature of the home's passive solar design.

Colorful blue furnishings in the living room, *opposite,* are a crisp contrast to the pristine white backdrop. Prettiest of all, and most complementary to the mellow country antiques, are the sky-blue sheets used for easy-care slipcovers on the sofa trio. Blue hues echo from the artwork and accents, including Susan's blue-and-white ware, collectibles that first inspired the couple's fondness for this tranquil color scheme.

Rather than inundate the room with an abundance of country antiques, the Connellys chose to dramatize the presence of several carefully selected pieces. Two standouts are the handsome pine armoire and the Mennonite dining table.

continued

Country Blues
In Southwest Harmony

Before it was remodeled, the Connellys' kitchen was small, dark, and decidedly lacking in style. Their new eat-in kitchen, *left*, offers all the amenities that a country cook could want, plus an inviting seating area, *above*. Susan set out to create "a functional and pretty kitchen that is a comfortable place to have family and friends around while I am cooking."

Once a laundry, the new sitting room has a nostalgic mix of old and new wicker, cushioned in country prints. Multiple windows, added for passive solar efficiency, produced a bonus: a spectacular view of distant mountains and ski slopes.

The kitchen work area incorporates a center island that is actually an antique cabinet topped with a slab of marble. The favorite cabinet has traveled with the Connellys from home to home. Also country in character are the custom-made, glass-fronted cupboards, fitted with panels of softly shirred provincial-print fabric.

The casual dining area is simply furnished with rush-seat ladder-back chairs around a blue-skirted table. An antique chest is used to store linens and tableware. The wrought-iron chandelier, with charming individual shades, is a French-country reproduction.

The Country Home
A House Stenciled With Style

Although it looks typically midwestern from the outside, this turn-of-the-century Missouri farmhouse, *right,* is steeped in New England colonial style. Owners Jeanie and Jim Benson are inveterate collectors of early Americana, and their house is filled with more than two decades' worth of wonderful finds.

A stenciling expert, Jeanie has embellished the family's suburban home in St. Louis with her hand-painted designs, creating a one-of-a-kind showcase for these cherished antiques. For the floral floorcloth on the home's porch, *above,* Jeanie chose a popular early-1800s stencil called "Summer Parlor."

continued

40

Every room in the Bensons' comfortable home displays the stenciling skills for which Jeanie is noted as a teacher and a restorationist. In the living room, *left,* a traditional pineapple motif, the familiar colonial symbol of welcome, adorns three walls at the ceiling line. The stencil colors—gold, deep red, and Williamsburg blue—are repeated, *above,* in the Oriental rug, the wing chairs' flame-stitch upholstery, and the charming window swags.

This inviting room has a congenial mix of antiques. Among the couple's favorites are the double desk behind the sofa and the circa-1880 pine school table, now used as a coffee table that displays a grouping of old brass candle holders. A bucket bench from the 19th century is a showcase for their collection of stoneware crockery. *continued*

Along with the decorative stenciling, the Bensons used rich colors extensively and effectively to enhance the colonial theme. In the dining room, *left,* Williamsburg blue makes an appropriate backdrop color for the setting of primitive American furniture.

Particularly charming are the Missouri-pine farm table and companion lyre-back chairs, dating from 1840. Beneath the window is a circa-1885 pie safe, now used for storage.

Assorted country collectibles lend colonial-era flavor to this convivial dining space. Tucked into a corner, the Pennsylvania pewter cupboard, *above,* is among the couple's most treasured country pieces. Beautiful in its rustic simplicity, the 1830s cupboard has chamfered doors and some original glass. *continued*

A House Stenciled With Style

(continued)

A t first glance, wall covering seems to provide the floral borders and intricate motifs in the Bensons' master bedroom, *below.* But the design is, once again, the masterful work of Jeanie and her paintbrush. The elaborate stencil treatment took her 81 hours to complete, and the overall design combines many different patterns. All are traditional stencils by Adele Bishop, a Vermont expert credited with today's renewed interest in stenciling, an art that dates to 2500 B.C. Egypt.

Brown, blue, and red hues in the stenciling reflect the room's warm woods and the colorful quilts topping a four-poster rope bed that was crafted of cherrywood in 1850.

On the home's third floor is daughter Pam's cozy attic bed-room, *below*, delightfully deco-rated with early American furniture. The wall covering's delicate floral print inspired the charming design that Jeanie stenciled in borders around the wood floor and on the muslin curtains. Antiques here include a Jenny Lind spool bed, a turn-of-the-century oak chest, and an 1880 Abe Lincoln-style desk with a drop front and cubby-holes. Adding to the room's old-time ambience is a collec-tion of antique dolls. *continued*

The Bensons' sunny kitchen, *right,* has a friendly farmhouse feeling, tempting all comers to settle on the ladder-back chairs or comfy loose-cushion sofa and make themselves at home. The 1840s pine table, with a two-board top and matchstick legs, adds a convenient work surface, and also serves for casual dining.

Design elements enhancing the farmhouse flavor include wide-plank wall paneling, crisp country-style tab curtains, and the authentic-looking *faux* brick floor, topped with a stenciled floorcloth. Old baskets, blue tinware, and a cupboard full of yellowware, *above,* play to the down-home mood. Rather than replace the 1940s metal cabinets, the Bensons updated these functional oldies with stenciling and butternut-color paint. Clear varnish protects the cabinets' finish from splatters and smudges inevitable in a hardworking country kitchen.

Creating Country Style

Like an intricately pieced quilt that derives its beauty from perfection in detail, country room schemes succeed on the finishing touches— handmade rugs, homespun fabrics, wall coverings bright with yesterday's motifs, and charming accents such as stenciling. These design ingredients link today's rooms with the past, and welcome as warmly as this century-old rug, perhaps inspired by an ancestor of Tuxedo the cat.

Creating Country Style
Floor Artistry

Centuries ago, itinerant painters peddled their art door-to-door, embellishing the colonists' modest homes with original freehand designs and intricate motifs applied with hand-cut stencils.

Colorful, but often primitive in pattern, the hand-painted floor gave settlers an affordable decorating alternative to the day's expensive rugs.

Today, the painted floor, with its inherent folk art charm, is a masterstroke of country style. Whether it is a simple checkerboard, a freehand "family tree," or authentic stenciling copied from a historic home, it adds nostalgic accent and individuality to a room scheme.

Design sources include museums and historical sites offering vintage stencils in do-it-yourself kits. The "Summer Parlor" pattern, popular in the early 1800s, is replicated on the quilting room floor, *right.* The stencil, painted in acrylics, tops a beige base coat of flat latex. Then, the floor was sealed with multiple coats of polyurethane. You also can use contemporary kits, or custom-design and cut stencils from commercial stencil paper, acetate, architect's linen, kraft paper, softwood, or tagboard.

Consulting restoration professionals is another option. The soft-brown stencil pattern on the farmhouse floor, *left,* was designed and executed by a professional artist. The stenciling complements motifs on the American Empire desk.

Simple methods, practice, and the right materials can assure project success. After sanding or cleaning the wood floor, measure it and calculate the design's repeat pattern. Use fast-drying acrylic paints and round, flat-tipped brushes. Remove excess paint from the brush by pouncing it up and down on newspapers or paper toweling until the brush is nearly dry and the paint almost powdery. Anchor the stencil with masking tape, hold the brush perpendicular to it, and paint with an up-and-down motion, working from the stencil edge toward the center. When the stenciling is dry, seal the floor with multiple coats of protective polyurethane.

Floor Artistry

(continued)

Stenciled in Shaker-red and cream-colored paints, the checkerboard floor, **right,** adds visual impact to the small entryway and offers visitors a decorative clue to this country home's interior.

The welcoming design was achieved with 8-inch squares, stenciled on the diagonal and surrounded by a painted border. Small floral motifs, in black and brown, accent each of the red squares.

Inspired by the abundant orchards surrounding this farm home, the primitive rendering of an apple tree, **right,** creates a cheerful focal point in the once-ordinary entry hall.

Enhancing the design's folk art appeal is a border of leafy vines and golden sun symbols. In addition to personalizing this on-the-floor masterpiece with the homeowner's name, the artists proudly signed and dated it.

Embellishing the curved stairway in an 1820s log house, the stenciled runner, **above,** combines vintage charm with the tough wearability demanded in high-traffic areas.

Lacy floral motifs accent the patina of the stairway's old wood, but the hand-painted design is protected under durable coats of polyurethane.

Finding a rug
appropriate in size,
shape, and color for
this French country
dining area could
have been difficult.
But, using custom-
designed stencils, a
professional artist
created this room-
size "rug," **left,**
inspired by the
pretty floral fabric
chosen for the
tieback draperies
and the chair pads.

The painted
flowers are set off
by an octagonal
border that outlines
the angles of the
windowed bay and
frames the
octagonal, glass top
of the dining table.

First, the
hardwood floor was
pickled, and then
sealed. The flower-
strewn border
design was applied
with oil-base paints.
After the stenciling
was dry, the artist
added two coats of
polyurethane as a
protective finish.

The pastel stencil
treatment combines
with graceful
furnishings, such as
the see-through
tabletop and ladder-
back chairs in
provincial style, to
set the room's airy,
gardenlike mood.
Even the chandelier
was painted in the
floral design used
on the floor.

Creating Country Style
Rustic Rugs

Prized today for their soft colors, practical warmth, and simple motifs, country rugs are a homespun legacy of thrifty pioneers. Short on supplies for fancier floor coverings, early settlers fashioned sewing remnants and rags into rugs, woven, braided, and hooked through burlap-sack backing. The most elaborate of these handcrafted coverings is the hooked rug, produced by centuries-old techniques that English and Scottish immigrants introduced to New England in the early 1800s. Worked with a primitive hook made of wood, bone, or forged

metal, these appealing rugs are valued for their original designs. After the Civil War, however, rug burlap came with preprinted patterns, and busy settlers lost interest in drawing their own rug designs.

On the country porch, *opposite,* old hooked rugs illustrate typical themes—geometrics, florals, and pictorials, especially those with birds, animals, and symbols of everyday life. The hexagonal rug is thought to be a "penny rug" for which an early 19th-century penny served as a template for the design's myriad circles. Common items, such as teacups and bricks, also were traced for rug patterns. The shaggy checked rug, on the porch rail, was made of hand-knitted wool hooked onto open-mesh burlap backing. The horn-of-plenty design in the circa-1880 rug, *below,* is worked in pastel-hued yarns.

Creating Country Style
Stencil Stagecraft

The stylized backdrop of the cozy family room, *left,* in an artist's Maryland home pays fanciful tribute to the age-old craft of stenciling.

More than historic embellishment befitting the casual mix of antique furnishings, the original hand-painted motifs are actually hardworking design elements, adding pleasing color and accentuating the architecture.

Though a variety of patterns combine in this floor-to-ceiling design, common colors link the diverse stencils and imbue the room scheme with fresh charm. An artful floral motif defines the woodwork, door jambs, and brick fireplace inset. Stenciled baskets, brimming with flowers, crown the double doors and each window, where even the simple tab curtains have hand-painted detail.

Stenciled around the room's perimeter, at the ceiling line, is a deep-green-and-rust border of vines that flares into half-fan motifs at the corners. Adapted from an old design in a book on historic homes, a bloom-and-leaf border, evident at the hearth, edges the room's hardwood floor. The floor was stained in a slightly darker tone to showcase the stenciling.

On the hearth's fireboard, the rustic landscape was painted freehand, then stenciled animals and country buildings were added by the artist.

Long before sophisticated wall coverings became a decorating option, stenciling added color and spirited detailing to colonists' simple homes. Custom-cut stencils can borrow motifs from fabrics, furniture, and other design elements, making this venerable craft a timely technique for personalizing and unifying today's country room schemes.

In creating the wall stenciling in the storybook bedroom, *above,* the homeowner-artist used a simplified version of the lovely painting and carving on the 19th-century Biedermeier-style bed. The running scroll pattern was adapted from the headboard's carved-leaf border, and the ribbon-tied bouquets from its painting. Separate stencils were used for each color. Motifs for stencils can be suc-

cessfully enlarged by photostating or mechanically reproducing them on a larger grid.

The stylized flower-basket stenciling that highlights the fireplace, *opposite,* was inspired by the antique chalkware on the mantel. For a softer, more primitive, look in keeping with this dining room's farm-style furnishings, the stencil painting was done with sponges instead of brushes.

Country Calico and Chintz

Extravagantly flowered and brightly studded with tiny motifs, captivating country prints are the most versatile of design ingredients.

In accents from window treatments to slipcovers, calicoes that dressed the American frontier, and chintzes, long a hallmark of European interiors, imbue country rooms with unrivaled spirit and charm.

Glorious samples of today's calico and chintz, *right,* carry on a decorative tradition begun in 14th-century India, where dyers perfected methods of permanently coloring cotton cloth. In the 1600s, traders brought the exotic fabrics to the Western world. From 19th-century India, the cotton fragment, *above,* is from Cooper-Hewitt Museum, The Smithsonian Institution's National Museum of Design in New York City.

Country Calico
And Chintz
(continued)

With the familiar, small-patterned design of today's country calicoes, the cotton fragment, **left,** is from 15th-century India. The eight-point stars and dotted ground were printed with pattern blocks. Found in Egypt in the late 1800s, it is part of the Textile Museum collection in Washington, D.C.

Forerunner of the glazed cotton cloth known today as chintz, the hand-painted bed cover, **above,** comes from India's Coromandel Coast in the first half of the 18th century. It is in Fries Museum, Leeuwarden, The Netherlands.

A design source of contemporary calicoes, the block-printed fragment, **below,** is a 19th-century Indian floral with white fleabane on a yellow-cream background. It is in the Cooper-Hewitt Museum collection in New York.

With numerous floral motifs combined with geometric shapes, the elaborate design on the cotton table cover, **left,** rivals the most intricate of modern pieced and quilted handiworks. Produced in the 18th or early 19th century in Rajasthan, India, the detailed design of the textile exemplifies the diversity of early print-block designs. It is part of the National Museum collection in New Delhi, India.

By the mid-1600s, Europeans considered the lightweight and washable Indian cotton something of a miracle fabric. European buyers fancied the designs, produced by stamping or drawing motifs on the cloth, then immersing the cloth in color-producing chemical baths, bleaching, and waxing.

Showing the dyers' intricate artistry, the fabric, *below,* is a detail from a late-18th-century Indian bed cover, composed of 1,040 block-printed squares and 1,038 different designs. It is from The Textile Museum in Washington, D.C.

By the early 1800s, Europe developed more sophisticated processes for making the glazed chintz and down-home calico fabrics that haved endured as country-style favorites.

Creating Country Style
Wall Covering Designs

Whether you want to imbue a room with the warmth of early Americana, the coziness of English country, or the old-fashioned romantic notions of Victoriana, country-style wall coverings beautifully imprint your personal style.

The most difficult decorating decision, initially, is choosing the appropriate mood-setting wall covering from today's profusion of designs. But by defining the look you want and considering your room's architectural elements, furnishings, and design needs, you can make a perfect match.

Playing to country's myriad moods, the wall covering array includes trellis patterns, tavern checks, garden-fresh florals, regimental stripes, miniprints, and interpretations of some historical designs such as the samples, *right.* The top examples are reminiscent of early stenciled motifs, the middle papers have the blue-and-white charm of Delft china, and the bottom samples echo the floral elegance of chintz fabric.

In the charming country setting, *opposite,* the pattern of the traditional stripes-and-floral wall covering and ceiling-mounted border carry out the woodwork's natural hue. The patterned backdrop softens the rustic lines of the vintage furniture gathered for this intimate hearthside dining spot.

Wall Covering Designs

(continued)

Since companion fabrics and mix-and-match borders come with many wall coverings, you can use pattern and color to unify a country room scheme. Fashioned into window treatments, slipcovers, pillows, and tablecloths, matching fabrics can give rooms a color boost and a pulled-together look.

Borders, too, are a versatile design element. They can be used to widen a window, create a frieze at ceiling level, or define architectural elements, such as a fireplace. Instead of traditional moldings, paper borders alone can be applied to walls at chair rail height for design interest in a plain room. For added definition, the paper, chair-rail border can be banded top and bottom by stock wood molding.

Wall coverings can give a fresh, flawless finish to old walls and visually enhance the scale of a too-small room or a too-high ceiling. In choosing the right wall covering, wearability, washability, removability, and cost are common considerations.

Country wall coverings should be compatible with vintage furnishings and a room's architectural elements, such as brick and wood-paneled walls and exposed beams. The sampler, *right,* shows a range of country wall coverings you can use to establish varied moods from the more formal allover florals to the casual plaid pattern and nostalgic miniprints.

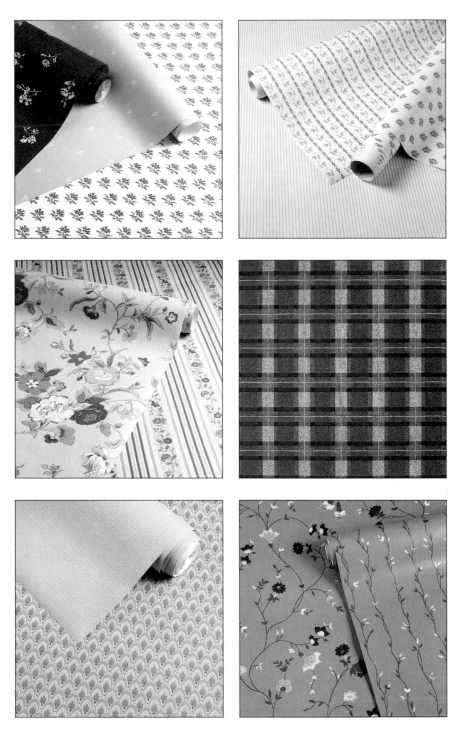

Wall coverings' versatility in setting a country stage is evident in the charming bedroom, *below,* in a cobbler's cottage two centuries old.

With a low sloped ceiling and original rough-hewn beams, the diminutive room needed a splash of color without large-scale pattern that would have overwhelmed the tiny space and upstaged antique furnishings.

The homeowner's solution was a terra cotta wall covering, sprinkled with tiny white dots. Applied between the beams, the wall treatment's soft color and crisp pattern cheer the rustic room. The white ceiling shows off the open beams and visually enlarges the space. The room is set with an antique iron bed, old pine pieces, and collectible hats, art, and textiles.

Country Furniture

To own a piece of handcrafted country furniture is to share in a sincere act of artistry. Honest in design and bold in spirit, these pieces were created to serve and endure, but early craftspeople were too proud of their skills to let utility alone guide them. The gracefully turned spindles on a chair, the grain-painting on a blanket chest, or the primitive carvings on a table attest to their desire for beauty in the home. By preserving these treasures, we honor our common ancestry.

This late-1700s Windsor armchair, **left**, has a comb back and typical chamfered seat, splayed legs, and H-shaped stretcher. The curved top rail ends in carved spirals, or ears. Generally, chair value is measured in spindles, with seven spindles most common and 11 spindles rare.

Country Furniture
A Windsor Quintet

An early-1700s import from England, the graceful spindle-back Windsor was colonial America's chair of choice. Thomas Jefferson is said to have penned the Declaration of Independence in a Windsor. The moniker is often credited to England's King George I, who ordered Windsor Castle craftsmen to copy the classic.

*An ingenious adaptation no doubt welcomed by early scholars, scribes, and statesmen, the Windsor chair, **above**, dated 1791–1817, has a flat writing, or tablet, arm incorporated into the arm rail. Windsors usually combined sturdy and resilient woods, then were painted to mask the mix. This Philadelphia-made piece includes tulipwood, maple, and chestnut.*

*Comfortable and so affordable that 1796 shopper George Washington purchased 27 chairs at $1.78 each for Mount Vernon, Windsor classics were also scaled down for children. The vintage 1765–1810 trio, **left**, includes a high chair, a child's armchair, and a tiny bow-back side chair only 11¼ inches tall.*

Shaker Simplicity

Patience and perfection guided Shaker furniture makers, for those virtues glorified God. Founded in 1776 by English immigrant Ann Lee, the Shaker religious sect that thrived in 19th-century America is renowned for its beautifully simple and functional designs. Priced around $1, their slat-back rocking chair first reached a secular market about 1790. The Shakers' majestic high chests inspired contemporary wall storage systems.

*From the late 1700s to the early 1900s, New Lebanon, New York, Shakers produced slat-back rockers, like the one **at left**, for their brethren and a secular market. With carved acorn-shape finials and simple turnings, the plain rockers, often of maple, shunned any worldly ornamentation as much as their makers did. Seats typically were woven rush, splints, or fabric strips. At chairside, the "sewing steps" allowed the Shaker seamstress a comfy footrest.*

*A testament to Shaker efficiency, the dual-purpose "table with drawers," **left**, tops storage with work space. Of oak and maple, it is signed by its maker: "D.W. Jan 1846." As on Shaker chests, drawer fronts are plain rectangles with turned button knobs. Even the small wooden box on top has a handy hidden drawer.*

The Shakers aptly dubbed the swivel chair, **above**, the "revolver" because it rotates on a screw pivot. In the 1800s, Shakers crafted them in New Lebanon, New York, where this maple-and-willow example likely originated between 1850 and 1875.

Set upon a molded base, the high chest, **above**, was made at Massachusetts' Hancock Shaker community. A handwritten note, found glued inside, reads: "This Case of Drawers were made by Elder Grove and Brother Thomas and placed here thursday, January 13th, 1853. It was the day our Ministry expected to return to the City of Peace, but were detained on anccount of the snow storm which occured on that day." Crafted of pine with butternut drawer fronts and walnut pulls, it bears traces of yellow stain.

An ancestor of today's bathroom sink, the simple washstand, **left**, typifies the precision construction and utilitarian beauty of Shaker furniture. Made of butternut, tiger maple, and pine, this circa-1850 necessity has snug joints and a tightly fitted drawer and door in the storage cabinet.

*Topped with a red-and-yellow painted checkerboard, the circa-1870 table, **right**, was probably originally crafted as a lamp or bedside table. Such game boards offered popular sport in early homes and inns. These square-top tables were common, but this midwestern piece has notable Sheraton-style legs added to the case exterior. Woods in painted pieces may be hard to identify and are sometimes determined by weight or by geographical origin.*

Painted Woods

Early furniture was painted to camouflage humble or mixed woods, accent special details, protect softwood surfaces, and mimic fancy European finishes. Today, original paint increases the value and folk charm of treasured country pieces.

*Almost seven feet long, the mid-1800s pine settee, **below**, was originally painted*   *blue. It borrows the slender lines of Sheraton style and has tapered legs and spindles reminiscent*   *of Windsor pieces. The seat is a single plank, and the curved arms end in deep scrolls.*

*Grain painting was a popular 19th-century technique used on humble pieces to imitate expensive woods such as mahogany and rosewood. In country Chippendale style, the circa-1860 pine chest, **above**, boasts a newly painted finish, its graining achieved by using combs, sponges, and age-old methods.*

At the heart of the pioneer home was the keeping room hearth, where the family gathered for cooking and dining. With storage usually minimal, chimney cupboards were handcrafted to keep essentials such as pots, pans, and utensils handy.

Custom-made to fit the odd-size niches beside the chimney, these useful cupboards were necessarily tall and narrow.

The circa-1840s chimney cupboard, **right**, more than six feet tall and a mere 11 inches wide, is made of poplar and pine. It bears its original red and blue-green paint, and it is topped with a heavy crown of 13-inch-wide molding.

Red paint disguises the hardwood mix in the spindle-back side chair, **left**, circa 1840. The spindles are probably made of hickory and the seat of maple. The chair's slender lines reflect a countrified rendition of the more formal Sheraton furniture style, popular in the late 18th century.

To supplement scant storage in early homes, cuches for everything from sugar and grain to a bride's dowry of linens were handcrafted in wood. Originally painted blue, the pine blanket chest, **right**, has beaded edging on the top and traces of stenciling on the scalloped skirt.

Country Furniture
Pioneer Crafted

On the journey westward, pioneers carried only a few cherished possessions sturdy enough to weather the rough wagon ride. They filled their new, primitive homes with simple, hand-hewn furniture, personalized pieces reflecting the strength, individuality, and honesty of their makers.

The tavern table's wide, flat top, well suited to food preparation, made it a favorite in the 18th and early 19th centuries.

*Set upon sturdy stretchers, the pine tavern table, **above**, is circa 1780. Two planks form the top, and the drawer probably stored cutlery and other utensils.*

*In colonial times, children's furniture followed prevailing styles in miniature, and the makers crafted special love and care into each piece. Double finials on the circa-1790 child's chair, **left**, are characteristic of*

the 18th-century designs. Blue paint, now chipped from wear, is evident on the chair's maple posts, hickory stretchers, and back slats, made of pine.

*Wooden Bible boxes stored family valuables in early American homes. The late-18th-century chest, **above**, is paneled pine with a simple design scratched in the gray paint.*

Actually a writing box pegged atop a simple frame, the pine slant-top desk, **right,** has pigeonholes and storage drawers beneath the hinged lid. A common mid-19th-century style, this piece has original green paint and a shallow, gallery edge to keep papers and books from slipping off.

A design of medieval origin, the dual-purpose settle or hutch table, **left,** proved a space-saver in tiny homestead rooms. This mid-19th-century pine piece, with original gray paint, has a movable top, held in place by dowels. When not used as a table, the top was tilted up to form the back of a benchlike seat. In drafty rooms, high-back settles were drawn close to hearths to reflect the warmth.

Primitive chip carving, in a circular pattern, embellishes the circa-1820 bench, **right,** set upon six gracefully tapered legs in tripod style. On the pine top, the design was achieved by using a knife or chisel to make diagonally opposed gouges. This painted bench is thought to be of Pennsylvania German origin.

Country Furniture
High Chairs
And Cradles

Lovingly crafted to lilliputian scale, early furniture made for children featured the charming details of the day's fashionable styles. High chairs, especially, mimicked adult furniture. Today, vintage cradles are prized for their enduring function and sentimental appeal. These pint-size pieces also make appropriate showcases for displaying childhood collectibles.

*A common 19th-century style, high chairs such as the slat-back example, **left**, seated generations of country youngsters. Simple in design and solid in construction, this circa-1840 piece bears remnants of its original blue paint. The footrest was probably a later addition or replacement.*

*A rope web forms the springs on this mid-18th-century cradle, just as it did on the adult-size colonial bed. Believed to be of Pennsylvania origin, the red-painted cradle, **left**, has primitive stenciled motifs similar to those used by the region's settlers to decorate their possessions, from household boxes to barns.*

80

Though cradle styles have varied little through the centuries, it is the small details that invest these miniature beds with such charm. Crafted in the early 1800s, the Shaker-style cradle, **right**, has a bentwood bonnet to protect baby from drafts. The side knobs anchored ties, securing the infant with an early equivalent of today's seat belts. A red stain blankets the pine frame.

Immigrant craftsmen brought homeland styles and woodworking techniques to the New World, combining them with native American materials to create distinctive colonial furniture. Made circa 1780, the infant's chair, **left**, shows a French influence in its chamfered legs, fancifully curved arms, and woven-splint seat. It is made of hickory.

The spindle-back Windsor chair was so popular that it was restyled into numerous pieces, even high chairs. Windsor elements are seen in the painted example, **above**, from the late 19th century. The chair's front stretchers and legs are simply turned, and a scalloped crest tops the back rail.

81

Country Furniture
Keeping Room Staples

Country keeping rooms and kitchens embraced a range of essential furnishings that were as hardworking as the people who used them. Ruggedly handcrafted, special-use pieces such as pie safes, jelly cupboards, dry sinks, and sugar chests indulged early homemakers with primitive convenience. Today, these pieces add vintage appeal to almost any room in the house.

*Even the smallest country kitchen likely had a pie safe for cooling and storing fresh-baked foods. Usually pierced-tin insets allowed for ventilation, and, today, intricate pierced designs— especially of animals and other figures— add value to a piece. **Above**, simple stars decorate the panels on a cherrywood pie safe, circa 1840.*

*From a southern plantation kitchen, the biscuit table, **right**, cleverly combines work space, utensil storage, and a protective cover for rising dough. After biscuits were rolled out on the poplar slab, the hinged top was closed over them. The pre-Civil War piece is primarily yellow pine and oak.*

Dry sinks, low cupboards usually topped by zinc-lined wells, held buckets and basins of water for household chores. Like the mid-19th-century example **above**, dry sinks were typically made of pine, an abundant wood source that cabinetmakers found especially easy to craft. Behind the cupboard door, there was storage or, often, a pail to catch drainage from a hole in the well.

With its multipurpose space-saving design, the early-20th-century oak cupboard, **right**, is almost a one-stop kitchen in itself. The glass-paneled doors conceal dish storage, the center doors front small pantries, drawers keep utensils handy, and the side cabinet is roomy enough for pots and pans. There's even a pull-out zinc counter.

The family-size dining table, **left**, is an example of turn-of-the-century golden oak furniture that remains popular today. The stout center leg provides extra support when leaves are added to double the length of this 4x4-foot square table. Such clean, functional designs blend beautifully with contemporary furnishings.

The corner, or roundabout, chair was made through many style periods and consequently can be found with a variety of plain and fancy turnings, splats, and spindles. The simple country version, **left**, circa 1780, has the basic cutout arm wrapping two sides of the chair.

Tables And Chairs

A testament to the industry of early woodworkers is the variety of chairs and tables that served settlers' homes. Between the 17th and 19th centuries, these craftsmen produced more than 100 different styles, from the primitive three-legged chair and crude trestle table to the painted Hitchcock chair and elegant Pembroke table. Many styles were copied from traditional European designs, but American hands transformed them with flair and imagination into works uniquely their own.

The mid-19th-century chair, **right**, is low to the ground and may have served for chores such as apple sorting. It has Shaker-style tapered legs, a splint seat, and acorn finials.

The simplicity of Sheraton style, popular in the late 1700s, appealed to rural artisans who copied the look into the 19th century. A Sheraton-inspired design, the drop-leaf table, **left**, crafted about 1825–1840, has a pine top that is artfully painted to mimic the burled grain of more costly flame mahogany used in formally styled pieces.

*Gateleg tables, so named for the swing-out legs that support drop leaves, were common in late-17th-century New England keeping rooms. Space-savers when folded flat, gateleg tables, such as the circa-1700 example **above**, have legs and stretchers turned in a classic vase-and-ring design.*

*Though crafted throughout the country, turn-top tables, such as the 1850–1870 example **below**, were found more often in southern homes. This Georgia pine table has a convenient lazy-Susan tray at the center.*

*Combining the vase-shape splat and curved back of American Queen Anne style with the turned legs, stretchers, and carved feet of the William and Mary period, the maple chair **above**, circa 1720s, exemplifies transitional design. Though city tastes changed, country craftsmen kept copying details from earlier periods.*

Country Furniture
Rocking Chairs

In conjuring up heartwarming images of country life, the rocking chair has few rivals. An early hybrid of cradle rockers and the straight chair, this comfortable and comforting seat remains the porch-and-fireside favorite of young and old.

*The fiddle-back rocking chair earned its name from the violin shape of its back splat. Decorated with painted motifs done freehand and with stencils, the chair, **above**, dates to the mid-1800s, the period when such pieces first became popular. Typical of the design, it features a curved top rail, a rolled seat, and turned legs and stretchers.*

*An emancipated slave, Missouri chairmaker William Kunze took his name and learned his trade from a German farmer who befriended him. With pointed finials, narrow slats, and wide arms, the circa-1800 chair, **right**, exemplifies the designs he worked exclusively in hickory.*

Arrow-back rocking chairs were named for the way the flattened back spindles taper into arrow shapes at the top rail. Typical of the design that was factory-produced from the 1860s to 1900, the mixed-wood chair, **above**, has a shield-shape seat and turned legs pegged onto the rockers' outer edges. A century ago, arrow-back chairs were popular for country bedrooms.

Antique furniture, even child-size pieces, from French-speaking parts of Canada is often as bold and rugged as the provincial terrain. With a sturdy rawhide seat woven like the sole of a snowshoe, the child's rocker, **left**, measures a mere 19 inches tall.

Intricately woven wicker furniture has been a perennial summer favorite since the late 19th century. Today, natural wicker is as elegant in the parlor as on the porch. The platform rocker, **above**, with a movable seat atop a stationary base, was designed to prevent rug wear. Its maze of curlicues, beautiful serpentine back, and comfortably rolled arms qualify this wicker rocker as a country classic.

Country Furniture
Bedroom Keepsakes

Reflecting the overall simplicity of early country homes, bedrooms were sparsely furnished and functional, usually appointed with small keepsakes from the marriage and a few heirlooms passed down through the family. Adding homespun accent and color to the spare surroundings were handcrafts such as colorful quilts that blanketed the bed's lumpy straw tick and stenciled motifs that brightened the room's requisite storage chests. These plain and practical pieces make comely additions to today's cozy sleeping spaces.

*Crafted of oak, the mirrored dresser, **left**, copies the graceful lines of American Empire furniture, a style that first gained popularity in the 1800s. This early-1900s example has the varied-size drawers and attached mirror typical of these pieces, mostly factory made.*

*A version of the armoire, the linen press was designed for household linen storage. Today, the versatile pieces are rare. The linen press, **left**, dated 1830–1850, is yellow pine, richly colored with umber graining over red buttermilk paint.*

*Colorful caches for hats and small trimmings, the pine boxes, **left**, are a legacy of Scandinavian-American craftsmen. All circa 1850, the top box is carved, the middle box has carved-and-burned motifs, and the bottom box is adorned with rosemaling, a form of folk-style freehand painting.*

Before the invention of the box spring and mattress, our ancestors slumbered atop straw-filled ticks supported by rope lattice. Such sturdy rope beds were a common comfort in the 19th century. Around the bed's perimeter, the ropes were anchored to the rails by holes or small knobs.

This 1860s youth bed, **below**, has rope supports and a classic spool design, so named because the footboard has turnings that resemble thread spools laid end to end. Early spool beds ranged from the primitive to the refined, depending on the craftsman's skill and the wood used. This rough-hewn bed has traces of original green paint and a simple flower motif beneath the crest rail.

The Hepplewhite-style chest, **above**, appears to have five storage drawers. But, this circa-1810 piece is actually a blanket box over two workable drawers on the bottom. The top three sections compose a false front, and the hinged top lifts to reveal space for blanket storage. This country-crafted chest bears original red paint.

Country Stores

No matter what their labels or heritage were—Dutch kas, French armoire, Irish dresser—cupboards were essentials in early homes with scant storage. Today's practical treasures, these large pieces evolved from simple open shelving that was enclosed in a frame.

*Exquisitely ornamented in characteristic French provincial fashion, the mid-18th-century cupboard, **left**, has a handy pullout slide for buffet serving. There's ample practical storage behind its hand-hewn doors with horizontal paneling in cherry wood.*

*The Irish cupboard, **above**, has a generous counter for dressing, or preparing, food. Thus, it is often called a dish dresser. In typical Irish style, it has a large rack and an open space at floor level for added storage. This mid-19th-century piece has chamfered doors beneath two narrow drawers for storing flatware.*

Thanks to their space-saving virtues, corner cupboards such as the mid-1800s example *at left* were exceptionally popular in early homes. In its original coat of blue paint, this yellow-pine piece from Georgia has delicate reeding on the front and a simple cornice, modest embellishments added by the country carpenter.

Because they were custom crafted to fit the nooks and crannies of early homes, cupboards come in myriad shapes and sizes, each unique in utility and beauty. The circa-1850 cupboard, *right,* is striking in the simplicity of its scrubbed-pine lines, plain moldings, and raised-panel doors.

Once the English oak piece, *above,* served as a tack or livery cupboard, a respository for harness needed by the manor house stables. Showing the design sophistication of its period, the circa-1720 cupboard is decorated with a series of raised front panels, underscored by twin drawers with rosette mounts and bail handles.

91

A Sampler Of Styles

*Talented Spanish carpinteros followed 16th-century conquistadors into New Mexico territory. Typical of their work are the rustic bench with cutout-back design, **left**, and the Spanish-style cupboard, **opposite, far right**, with American folk grain painting.*

The classic styles of country furniture are as numerous as the nationalities in America's great melting pot. Everyday pieces, ultimately crafted for comfort and utility, reveal the strong influences of ethnic heritage, regional tastes, native materials and crafts, and disparate aesthetic views. All combined to enrich the legacy of early furniture makers.

*Clean vertical lines and an intentional primitiveness mark pieces crafted in southern plain style. The early 19th-century cellarette or liquor stand, **right**, of yellow pine and walnut, is a chest on a frame. A decade ago, when it was moved for the first time this century, Confederate currency was found strapped to the bottom of the case.*

Listed as sugar stands or cellars on the inventories of old southern plantations, wooden chests held an early household luxury— sugar—and were crafted with fittingly fine detail.

*The mid-1800s sugar chest, **above**, is made of stained poplar and walnut and is secured by the original lock. Though these sugar stores were made throughout the country, they are among pieces found more frequently in southern homes.*

Noted for dark oak finishes, rectilinear stances, and straightforward materials, turn-of-the-century mission furniture is enjoying a renaissance of popularity today. A leader in American mission design, Gustav Stickley was influenced by Britain's late-19th-century Arts and Crafts Movement, a revolt against the industrial age and Victorian excess. The 1902–1903 Stickley chair, **top, left,** has, as subtle ornamentation, a V-shape back rail. Beauty and function are synonymous in his drop-front writing desk, 1905–1907, **bottom, left.** Inspired by furnishings found in a California mission, the mission label has become generic for simple handcrafted pieces.

Long after the popularity of folk styles waned in Europe, American immigrants wanted new furnishings reminiscent of the cherished pieces they left behind. More than 7 feet tall, the 19th-century cupboard, **above**, revives Germanic folk style. This example, in butternut wood, has narrow doors set between wide stiles.

Factory-made from the 1860s through early 1900s, American cottage furniture, with applied moldings, painted surfaces, and gilded or stenciled decoration, was an especially popular style for bedrooms. Rural craftsmen copied the common style, handcrafting it in beautiful variations. Produced in Missouri by German-American cabinetmakers, the white-maple washstand, **above**, and the walnut dresser, **right**, illustrate the delicate scale and carved adornments of these simple, but sturdy, pieces.

The single door and wide stiles of the 1840–1880 pie safe **at right** are common details of Germanic folk style. Crafted in cupboard form, it has ventilation holes bored on all sides for cooling and keeping baked goods. The square legs taper into cleats, and it has traces of original red paint.

Biedermeier furniture was characterized by a potpourri of classic features taken from French Empire, Sheraton, Regency, and Directoire styles. Biedermeier influence is evident in the wardrobe, **below**, with its raised-panel doors, diamond motif, and deep cornice.

America's rural cabinetmakers modified elegant forms of German Biedermeier furniture, made between 1815 and 1850. The Biedermeier-style chair, **left**, has curved back slats with fancy-cut mahogany veneer. Usually, such countrified chairs have outsweeping saber front legs and two back rails. The Biedermeier name comes from an imaginary German magazine character, typifying middle-class tastes.

Reproductions Today

Time and the zeal of country collectors have made antique furniture scarce, but yesterday's celebrated designs are available today in first-rate reproductions. Styles such as Shaker, Windsor, Queen Anne, and other colonial-era classics are being crafted in true-to-tradition form. In considering these timeless designs, it is important to remember that reproductions are line-for-line copies of original pieces, and adaptations are designs that have been slightly altered to accommodate modern needs.

*Replayed in reproductions, the clean lines and function of early pieces meld beautifully with contemporary country furnishings. The console table, **above**, has simple Shaker-style detail.*

*Interpretations of specialty pieces, such as corner chairs, tilt-top tables, armoires, and candlestands, make vintage charm affordable and available. Appropriate for today's small rooms, this adaptation of a Shaker tilt-top table, **above**, can be flipped up for a lamp or serving table, then folded flat and stored against a wall to save space. It is similar to Shaker tables of the mid-19th century.*

Though many facets of furniture making have changed since our ancestors first settled into Shaker rocking chairs, well-designed reproductions and adaptations succeed on the meticulous attention to detail that sometimes demands reviving age-old techniques. Perhaps the most beloved of Shaker pieces is the slat-back rocking chair, and the adaptation, **below**, has features faithful to the original—a checkerboard seat of woven fabric strips, mushroom caps on the arms, and simple back slats.

Collectibles Showcase

The legacy of common hands, country collectibles not only give tangible form to our fancies, but also cue images of simpler times. In an old sampler, we see the young pioneer girl stitching by the firelight. Amish textiles summon scenes of quilting bees with devout women working geometric puzzles in fabric. Country wares we lovingly use and proudly display remind us of early keeping rooms. And the hug-worn rag doll makes us ponder what growing up was like long ago.

Showing Off Treasures

For country flavor in this once-contemporary dining room, the homeowners chose appealing kitchen collectibles. An old corner cupboard is stocked with yellowware bowls, a favorite since the 1830s, and platters made of ironstone, a 19th-century ware prized for its clean lines and luster.

These venerable wares move to the hutch table for serving country-style buffets. Wooden butter molds, *above,* share a shelf with the yellowware.

A reminder that our ancestors, too, fought the wrinkle, toy flatirons and those once used for shirt collars are grouped together, *right.* The stand held irons for heating over a gas flame.

Collectibles Showcase
Country Wares

Redware's rich tones are so beautiful against the patina of aged wood that the owner of the mid-1700s Queen Anne dresser, *below,* instinctively matched the two old friends. Whether the grouping is extensive or small, showcasing like collectibles against a vintage backdrop guarantees impact.

The oldest form of American pottery, redware was first made in colonial New England and Pennsylvania. Its fragility has made redware rare and, though designed for early use, it is best suited for decorative display. Folk potters fashioned these plain and fancy plates and bowls of coarse red clay.

To create contrasting designs sometimes found on redware, potters trailed a diluted mixture of ground clay, lead, and other minerals, known as "slip," over the pieces. Since the 1600s Jamestown settlement, myriad items from roof tiles to whistles have also been made from the same plentiful clay.

Though everyday necessities such as pails and pans were made of tin, artists crafted a whimsical tradition with the humble material. The tin pieces, *below,* are the legacy of the charming 19th-century custom of celebrating a couple's tenth wedding anniversary with personalized tin gifts.

Today, the imaginative trifles are tokens of Victorian romance and the subject of often humorous speculation about the recipients. For example, imbibers or teetotalers may have been honored with the chalice, natty dressers may have gotten the top hat, and smokers may have received the pipe.

Collectibles Showcase
Country Corners

In the restoration of an 1830s farmhouse, this artistic homeowner considered every corner a blank canvas waiting to become a masterpiece. But her medium was collectibles. The intimate galleries that she created elevate her treasures to starring roles in appealing vignettes. Though the cast of collectibles may vary in size, number, or vintage, these artful arrangements can establish a room's country character or carry a period theme throughout the house.

A distinctive collection of framed samplers, most from the early 19th century, share the corner setting, *below,* with stenciled furniture. Combining the

samplers with the miniature Hitchcock settee and antique dolls seems appropriate because these endearing textiles were once an important part of a young girl's life. Commonly worked on unbleached or dyed linen, linsey-woolsey, or a gauzelike fabric called tiffany, samplers were the slate upon which girls learned the alphabet, numerals, and Bible verses while practicing their sewing. More elaborate than European designs, American samplers had intricate floral motifs, moral verses, family trees, pictorials, and rare, globe-shape maps.

The serene and sunny niche, *below,* is set with hand-painted pieces, pared from more extensive collections displayed throughout the farmhouse. The circa-1830 flax wheel, from Virginia, has original stenciling and the maker's signature. The Hitchcock settee, salt-glazed stoneware, and painted "bride's box" on the sill celebrate varying forms of early artistry.

Quilts On Display

Quilts are beloved for their singular homemade beauty and kaleidoscope colors and patterns that transcend their original purpose as warm bed coverings. Spread over a sofa, artfully displayed on a wall, or draped on a quilt rack, these high-spirited textiles convey a sense of warmth and comfort. Made in Kentucky between 1880 and 1900, the intricately pieced Star of Bethlehem, or Lone Star, quilt, *opposite,* forms a mosaic backdrop for vintage treasures in a country parlor.

Amish quilts, such as those *above,* are simple in design, but they are highly admired for their bold tones and geometric orderliness. Pledged to the plain life by the sect's religious dicta, Amish women found quilts an outlet for their creativity, and collective quilting bees were a rare chance for the women to socialize. Amish quilts are characterized by monochromatic borders, vivid colors, and superb quilting stitches in traditional diamond, tulip, and wreath motifs.

Childhood Cherishables

Loving hands created yesterday's dolls and huggable toys from leftovers—bits of homespun cloth, snippets of lace, stray buttons for eyes, and wisps of thread for smiles. Generations of children treasured them, and today's collectors prize them as true American folk art.

Friendly faces from the past charm young and old alike. Born this century, Raggedy Ann and Raggedy Andy dolls, **opposite,** at first had heart-shape faces, instead of round ones, and red celluloid hearts attached to their soft torsos. They were first made in 1920. Country dollmakers endowed their creations with personality and charming detail. In the group at **right, top,** the circa-1860 boy doll, seated in a tiny chair, has leather shoes and hair of beaver fur. Amish dolls typically had no facial features. The tiny Amish trio in the foreground on the right are sometimes called pocket dolls, sized to fit into a child's pocket. Made in varied materials from fancy bisque to dried apples, early black dolls, such as those at **right, bottom,** are popular collectibles. In the basket, the circa-1860 doll on the right has eyes of painted tin. The lady, seated behind in the chair, has a dried-apple face, a silk-and-lace dress, velvet shoes, and pearl-button eyes.

Childhood Cherishables
(continued)

The inherent enchantment of old playthings, lovingly arranged in a sentimental showcase, adds warmth and interest to a room. Child-size antique furniture is especially appropriate in these charming vignettes. The guest bedroom, **left**, has a corner on nostalgia, with its colorful collection of 19th- and 20th-century doll quilts displayed on the quilt rack and a handmade doll bed. These small patchworks were often made by country children learning stitchery skills. Generations of "Teddy's bears" find a fitting home in an early-1800s cradle, **opposite**. These irresistible stuffed toys gained American favor in 1902 as the namesakes of Theodore Roosevelt, who, on a much-publicized hunting trip, refused to shoot a bear cub.

Family Room Folk Art

From its old barn rafters to its weathered floorboards, the cozy family room, *right,* in a century-old New England farmhouse, brims with fanciful finds to delight the eye and the sense of humor. This uninhibited display celebrates the collectors' fondness for old toys.

Made this century by a Canadian artist who used salvaged scraps for his designs, the miniature fire truck, *above,* is from the room's folk fleet. These charming vehicles have hand-carved wooden passengers with movable arms and legs. Old game boards are grouped for colorful accent on the wall, and other pieces, such as a wooden Indian mailbox holder and the tin-steepled church on the sofa table, star solo.

Collectibles Showcase
A Fanciful Farmhouse

STOP METRIC MADNESS

Eighteenth-century shop- and innkeepers relied upon striking, sculptural advertisements to lure colonial customers who could recognize common trade symbols, but who often could not read. The lighthearted design of the farmhouse living room, *left,* combines those early signs with a witty array of treasures. The red wooden hand, dangling from the ceiling, once marked a glovemaker's shop, and the tin pocket watch, by the hearth, a clock shop.

Designed around a few bold pieces, this uncluttered, sparsely furnished space emphasizes how contemporary folk pieces can blend beautifully with vintage ones of the same flavor. True to the big-spirited lines of the oversize antiques, the miniature plane, *above,* commemorates the homeowner's great-uncle, who once built a real flying machine. Handcrafted by folk artists, weather vanes, such as the codfish perched on the mantel, have been popular forecasters since the 1700s.

Timeless Finery

Country collectors have embellished the old adage that home is where you hang your hat. Yesterday's frocks of silk and taffeta, hand-embroidered petticoats, child-size fashions, high-button shoes, and fancy bonnets now compose the vintage wardrobe sought for wearing and home display.

Expert stitching, luxurious fabrics, and intricate trims, such as beadwork, increase the value of early clothing. Conversely, alterations and fabric damage decrease worth. Vulnerable to light, humidity, dust, and wear, these fragile creations require special care in display and storage.

In the 1800s, bonnets were dictates of fashion, mores, and the weather. When women doffed their muslin nightcaps, they donned simple, cotton or lace morning caps.

Fancier millinery of stiffened silk, velvet, or tulle festooned with flowers, feathers, and ribbons saw them through the day's outings, and straw bonnets were a

*summer favorite. Arrayed on a shelf and a circa-1820, grain-painted chest, antique bonnets, **above**, add vintage appeal to the master bedroom in a 19th-century farm home. On the chest,*

beribboned and ruffled examples are displayed on a pair of French milliner's headstands. Antique straw bonnets have become rare collectibles.

Composed in charming vignettes worthy of still-life paintings or used as accents in a variety of hard-to-decorate spaces, antique apparel adds a warm touch and sense of history to a country room scheme. In a sliver of hallway between this home's master bedroom and kitchen, the tiny garments of yesterday's child, **top, right,** are imaginatively arranged against a white backdrop embellished with blue stenciling. The blue, Shaker-style peg rail holds baby shoes, knitted socks, and toddler-size overalls in denim. A vintage doll, old samplers, a decoy, and a basket with rolls of bright rug rags complete the setting.

In a home two centuries old, the plain, pine-plank wall, **bottom, right,** makes a great place to hang a broad-brimmed collection of hats. The soft, saucerlike shapes break up the expanse of horizontal lines, and the hats' ribbons and nosegays accent this top-of-the-stairs spot with color.

Collectibles Showcase
Gathering Favorites

Whether chosen for fun, fortune, beauty, or myriad other subjective reasons, vintage collectibles indelibly imprint personal style. Virtually anything is collectible, if you enjoy the chase or the look, and these treasures on display give every room one-of-a-kind charm.

Country collectors have a knack for seeing beauty in simple, everyday objects. Even old thread spools carry a torch in the illuminating group, *above.* Visitors to the 18th-century home, *top, right,* are greeted by an intriguing collection of old umbrellas, their fancifully carved handles sprouting from an urn in the entry hall. Though some treasures are strictly for display, others are beautiful, hardworking additions. Open shelves in the pantry, *bottom, right,* keep green Depression glass, yellowware, and baskets handy. Botanical prints add a fresh accent here.

Intricately embroidered and expertly stitched, the software that dressed ancestral bedchambers ranked among the prized possessions of early homes. Old estate inventories reveal that only land, buildings, and wrought silver exceeded quality textiles, such as bedding and bed curtains, in value.

No longer sleepers among collectibles, antique bed linens can be mixed with today's handcrafts and bedwear for a tempting heirloom look. Linens from the late 1800s and early 1900s are displayed on the carved bed, *below.* Early needle-workers favored the red-on-white theme because the bold

contrast made even the simplest of designs festive. The pillow embroidery was worked on damask and homespun cloth. The headboard quilt is a sun-flower pattern variation, and the bed quilt is a circa-1880s Wild Goose Chase pattern. These delicate textiles require special care in cleaning, storage, and display.

HENRI ROUSSEAU

Country
Interiors

From its rustic roots, country is blooming, like a cottage-garden kaleidoscope, in a variety of beautifully personalized interiors. Whether your decorating passion is rustic Americana, cozy English, or eclectic contemporary, country matches each mood with an emphasis on comfort and a reverence for the past. This city-style living room marries today's sleek seating and old favorites—dramatic quilts, antique collectibles, and primitive furniture—for a striking country look.

OF THE REAL
the Pieced Quilt

AMERICAN FOLK PAINTERS OF THREE CENTURIES

AMERICAN INDIAN ART

Country Interiors

New England Update

Set in beautiful counterpoint, a mix of family heirlooms, handmade treasures, and contemporary furnishings brings fresh country charm to this living room in a new colonial-style home in Connecticut. Facing off over the dhurrie rug, sleek low-back sofas, softened with plump country-print pillows, set a mood of casual comfort. The rug's pattern is reminiscent of pioneer patchwork.

Brushed in natural hues, this updated showcase is designed to give antiques and handmade pieces, such as the simple mantel and walnut coffee table, special recognition.

Around the Pennsylvania pie safe, *above,* and throughout the room, collections of aged duck decoys and old crockery have been astutely pared to highlight their singular beauty, and they have been clustered together for added impact.

123

Country Interiors
Farmstead Treasures

Lovingly collected during the restoration of a Virginia farmhouse, American antiques gracing this living room recapture the refined beauty of a century past.

In this narrow room, the massive hearth becomes the natural focus of a conversation area, where a stenciled Hitchcock chair and wing chair offer fireside seating. The stenciled settee, under the window, and the red wardrobe, dominating the far wall, are 19th century.

Remarkable among the distinctive pieces is the circa-1820s, grain-painted blanket chest, *above*. To achieve the chest's handsome design, the early craftsman applied brown paint with corncobs.

Bold Country Geometry

This country-inspired family room, in a newly built Wisconsin saltbox, interprets New England style with refreshing flair. Though imposing beams and antiques share roots in past centuries, such timeless elements meld with pale hues and bold accents in an up-to-date, yet rustically comfortable, look.

Defining the hearthside seating area, a dramatic floorcloth copies, on painted canvas, the classic Tumbling Blocks pattern of pioneer quilts. Other vintage patchworks splash color over the twin sofas, covered in easy-care ticking stripes. The 18th-century gateleg table serves as a cocktail table. In winter, sofas are dressed in crewel work covers, and an Oriental rug replaces the floorcloth.

The four-door wall cupboard, circa 1820s, stores today's home entertainment equipment and yesterday's stoneware. A few well-chosen collectibles—pull-toys on the mantel and a carved horse on a tavern table at the window—reflect the homeowners' love for animals.

To showcase their vintage collections, details of historic New England homes were replicated. The ceiling beams were salvaged from a century-old barn, and the fireplace is a version of one in a restored Deerfield, Massachusetts, home.

126

A Designer's Rustic Home

I n an 1815 log home nestled in the crook of a country lane, this keeping-room-studio was designed by a descendant of Ohio's pioneer vanguard. Old timbers, newly handcrafted furnishings, and a wealth of collectibles summon the warmth and comfort of a century past to this new addition.

Flanking a camelback sofa in the hearthside conversation area, the cozy wing chairs were produced by local craftspeople from the homeowner's designs. Homespun fabrics—tavern checks on the chairs and high-tie curtains and a stencillike pattern on the sofa—create cheerful contrast against the dark, dominant woods.

The large cupboard, *above,* built from salvaged wood, holds the bolts of cloth that are the designer's staples. When her work requires elbowroom, a three-board round table stands ready on the painted floor. The table and the floor's diamond design reflect her artistry.

Country Interiors
A Bungalow Renewed

G arden patterns and sherbet colors, in a mix-and-match celebration, work fresh country-cottage magic on this multipurpose family room in a renovated 1920s bungalow.

After old pillars and half-walls came down, enough luxurious space emerged to accommodate living and dining areas, separate in up-to-date function but equally beautiful.

Sunny fabrics wrap the sink-in seating, coordinating varied styles such as the overstuffed pieces and clean-lined contemporary sofa. Soft pillows, in matching fabrics, are plump and plentiful, extending comfortable seating options to the floor.

Background accents—wall covering, rag rugs, crown molding, and balloon window shades—are brushed with hues from the same romantic palette. An old bench serves as a coffee table and a wicker basket as chair-side storage.

A mix of rich woods and rustic textures in the dining area tempers the sweetness of the adjacent sitting spot. Around the generous-size antique table, the rush-seated chairs are of varied vintage. A pass-through from the kitchen to the dining area efficiently doubles as a buffet for entertaining.

An Enchanted Cottage

Beneath rough-hewn beams of a 220-year-old cobbler's saltbox, the romantic formality of this tiny living room emerges from a studied contrast of primitive woods, elegant fabrics, and collectibles. Woven together with common-denominator colors, seemingly disparate elements—rustic fishing baskets, gilt-framed art, and cool silks—imprint truly personal style.

Against a backdrop of dusty turquoise and crisp white, the rich rug and new frocks on old seating set a luxurious mood.

American primitive pieces earn new roles in this eclectic scheme. Canvas decoys and Staffordshire dogs are displayed on a painted cupboard and vintage table, paired in secretary style. An antique game table is now a coffee table.

Pleasing contrast carries to the corner, *above,* where an heirloom grandfather clock stands in carved splendor next to a humble coal tin that doubles as a lamp table and a bin for storing fireplace wood.

Country Interiors
City-Style Patchworks

Antique quilts granted fine art status kindle uncommon energy in the living room of this 1850s cottage, located in the restored German Village in Columbus, Ohio.

With a deft mix of old and new furnishings, this diminutive space gets a bold boost of color from an 1880s star quilt displayed on the aged brick wall. Revealing design foresight of early stitchers, graphic patterns in old textiles beautifully meld diverse elements—a traditional camelback sofa covered in canvas, contemporary chairs, and a painted antique blanket chest. Displayed between the crisp white shutters, *above,* is a 1930s quilt block, distinctive for its black background.

135

Romance With Collectibles

Brimming with Victorian spirit and a menagerie of whimsical accents, this cozy California parlor blooms in patterns and colors drawn from the country-garden print on the softly shirred sofas.

The homeowner picked exuberant pinks to unify the comfortable space. Crown moldings in white accent the blush tint on the walls, and the pink-and-white theme repeats in the plaid slipper chairs, soft window treatment, and rag rug.

Staffordshire dogs perch on the mantel and nestle with old teddy bears and dolls in the Irish pine hutch. More than decorative, the sturdy sheep, around the piano, *above,* serve as pull-up seats and footstools.

Handcrafted Elegance

The convivial charm of this new Connecticut dining room turns on the homeowners' ability to see beauty in humble country stock.

In this gallery of lamb's-wool-toned walls and honey-hued hardwood, the hospitality revolves around the chestnut-and-pine table hewed from corncrib remnants. The pine hutch, *above,* and chandelier are crafted of old iron and wood.

Reproduction Windsor chairs set tradition, and the dhurrie rug adds new color and textural contrast. Such a simple setting allows each handmade piece its proper air of importance. Heralding hospitality within, an heirloom desk stands beneath a contemporary seacoast scene.

139

Country Interiors

Contemporary Country Fare

S ince the 1800s, industrious farm families have been drawn from the fields to feasts around this rough-hewn harvest table. The cherished antique, crafted of Missouri-pine planks, now anchors a suburban setting as beautifully as it served the primitive farmstead kitchens of the past.

Reverently simple in design, this sun-dappled St. Louis dining room succeeds with a few fine pieces and collectibles carefully chosen for dramatic impact and unchallenged by clutter.

A recessed spotlight literally shines on a handsome 19th-century hooked rug, displayed on the wall like fine art. The rug is an intricately beautiful variation of the popular Log Cabin pattern often stitched into quilts. A smaller hooked rug serves as a table runner.

Once a cache for a winter's worth of edibles, the tall, pine canning cupboard still wears its original orange-red paint. Atop it, the Eastern Woodlands Indian baskets, with splints softly shaded in natural dyes, date to the turn of the century.

Beneath a primitive oil painting of water lilies, the maple-topped farm table serves as a sideboard when diners occupy the old, painted-pine chairs. Opposite it, the American chest, under framed watercolors of English village scenes, is of 1850s vintage.

Country Interiors
Hearthside Hospitality

Conjuring the true country enchantment of this cozy keeping room called for brewing aged ingredients in a new pot— a recent-vintage home inspired by 18th-century designs.

The authenticity of the room comes from recycled materials, such as old bricks for the fireplace, and custom crafting of door latches, moldings, hinges, and the tin light fixture.

Clad in Shaker red paint, wide, clear-pine paneling and a simple mantel frame the fireplace, a full five feet wide at the opening.

Like its colonial counterparts, the inviting hearth is a magnet for family gatherings. Ready to take advantage of the cheery warmth is an 18th-century New England hutch table, the top of which tilts back to form a settle. For dining, the table, bearing its original paint, is encircled with 19th-century Hitchcock-style chairs. A cooking crane, built into the fireplace, keeps kettles of hearty soups simmering.

The plank floor is stenciled in a colorful "area rug" of authentic colonial design. New ceiling beams are stained to resemble old, smoke-darkened timbers.

Completing the nostalgic mood is a harvest of accents collected from antiques shops and the family garden—pantry boxes, pewter ware, iron utensils, a flax wheel, and home-grown culinary herbs.

142

Cottage Rounds

With one simple stroke of geometry—an intimate round table decked for dining— any space can be transformed into a rustic country inn or charming English cottage. Colorfully skirted or left beautifully bare, the round table for two means memorable sunrise breakfasts, high teas, and midnight suppers.

The dining corner, *left,* blends timeless country motifs and textures in a contemporary setting. Unadorned walls and crisp white shutters showcase the graceful table and armchairs with backs reminiscent of a farmer's bushy wheat sheaf. Though the bold-checked rag rug is new, it has the classic charm of homespun.

Simple accents include a new brass lamp, aged candlesticks, and newly applied blue-and-white tiles, added to define the fireplace opening.

Basking in a bright bay window at the end of a large, more formal dining room, the cottage table, *above,* evokes coziness with an English accent. As fresh as a country garden, blossoms in persimmon, rust, and blue bloom over the chintz table skirt. Tieback draperies made of the same sunny fabric outline this inviting, intimate niche.

In contrast, antique Jacobean armchairs, which provide rather regal seating, are upholstered in soft blue plaid.

145

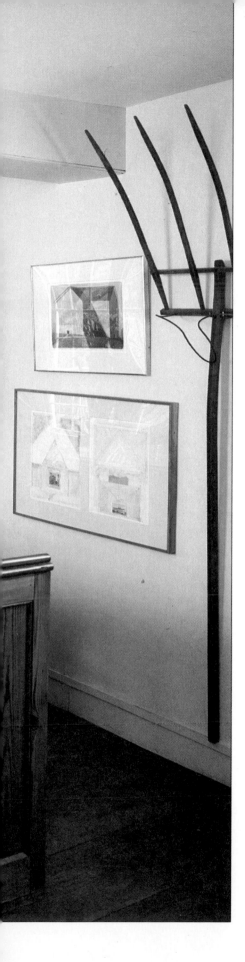

Country Interiors
Gathering Benches

Wooden benches stir images of the pioneer faithful at worship or little scholars sitting primly in a one-room school. They serve where people gather, suggesting a closeness and community sometimes lost on individual chairs. What better place for benches than at a gracious dining table.

In ecclesiastical order, church pews flank an old rectory table in this Connecticut farmhouse, *left*. But with warm woods, a sunny exposure, and witty display of the old hay fork, the room is lighthearted, not sol-emn. The amicable mix combines an English scrubbed-pine armoire and butternut sideboard with modern art.

In a 250-year-old Massachusetts home, the dining room, *above,* is a meticulous rendition of the colonial hall. With hooked rugs, mellow woods, and country wares, it has the warmth, function, and accents our ancestors prized.

The Shaker-style table was crafted from old floorboards. A hearth bench, "firehouse" Windsor chair, and Indiana cupboard add antique appeal. Quilts, pewter, and a bow rake reveal collectors' passions.

147

A Cordial Colonial

Primitive yet gracious, the dining room in this century-old New Hampshire farmhouse is a heartwarming blend of a family's personal treasures and their homespun artistry.

The cheery, hand-painted floor has folk art charm because some red diamonds, brushed onto the yellow base, are less than perfectly shaped. A duck parade, stenciled at the ceiling, and calico tab curtains echo the floor's country hues.

Rush seats on the Chippendale chairs are in casual counterpoint to the gracefully carved backs. An elegant accent is the massive heirloom bowl on the simple tavern table.

The child's portait, *above,* is one of several old canvases composing an extended country family. An old jelly cupboard holds a collectible favorite— American ironstone.

149

Simply Pine With Polish

In settings innovative yet comfortable, sophisticated yet casual, rustic pine furniture turns from country cousin into a room's elegant star.

This California dining room, *right*, offers an unexpected style mix. Etched glass and glazed walls say English drawing room, but the simple pine table and ladder-back chairs speak of country comforts. The tailored tieback draperies are canvas lined with cotton.

A white backdrop in the city "farmhouse," *above*, sets an elegant stage for a pine table and an old Welsh dresser laden with ironstone. Twig chairs and vine wreaths make earthy accents.

Country Interiors
French Flair
In the City

B lack, white, and bold, this dramatic Chicago kitchen minds its country manners in French style.

Glass-fronted cabinets, *right,* evoke images of the past, and match those in a quaint butler's pantry annexed in the kitchen makeover. Functional, and also appealing for collectibles display, the cabinetry, accented in gold hardware, enhances the airy openness of the space. In the sunny yellow dining area, *above,* a glass-top table also contributes to the room's light look by showing off the stretch of black-and-white tile beneath it. Overhead, the glass-shaded antique light fixture adds country charm.

Floral fabric, reminiscent of an intricately stitched Flemish tapestry, covers cushions on the provincial chairs, and frames the doorway in tieback curtains.

Country Interiors
Collectibles Gallery

Collectors naturally like to show off, usually with cupboards full of good reasons. And a generous helping of such treasures can elevate the humble galley into a singular gallery of old-fashioned charm.

In creating the nostalgic kitchen, *below,* the country cook reconciled seemingly incompati-

ble needs: efficiency for a bustling catering business and a showcase for beloved antiques. The solution subtracted a wall to add requisite space, and proves that high-volume cooking need not require a stark, high-tech environment.

Coordinated clutter—American primitives, baskets, crockery, cookbooks, and old utensils hooked to barn-wood beams—is a beguiling link between dining and work spaces.

In the dining area, 19th-century pine pieces set an old New England mood. The long "scrub" table, draped in paisley, is reserved for sit-down feasting. And the unusual apothecary chest, *below, right,* is a collector's dream, with ample nooks, crannies, and shelves for a multitude of crockery bowls, pots, and pitchers.

Haitian folk sculptures in steel are silhouetted in the window beyond the pine table and in the sunny bay window above the sink.

Country Interiors
A Colorful Contemporary

When contemporary and country meet in this kitchen, the result is a beautiful blend of warmth and verve. Modern in its complement of appliances, this spacious kitchen, nonetheless, reveals down-home country roots.

The meld is apparent in sleek, corn-silk-hued pine cabinetry. The wall covering recalls pioneer ginghams, and its watermelon-red brightens the pine table and bow-back chairs. Ceiling beams and the natural wood floor hint of rustic kitchens past. The clever addition, *above*, offers hang-up storage on the side-grid and shelves within.

Country Interiors
Distinctively European

Casual yet elegant, this old-world kitchen copies the fluent style and function of backstairs cookrooms found in gracious continental manor houses. But instead of serving a country chateau steeped in grand history, it embellishes a small, newly remodeled New Orleans home.

Recycled from old buildings scheduled for demolition, time-worn ceiling beams and the plank floor establish a venerable look that belies the addition's recent vintage. Antique flavor extends to the multipurpose tile-top island, a work and dining hub built of old timbers.

Up-to-date appliances provide efficiency, but the mellow woods and pale paint on the walls and island prevent metallic surfaces from dominating and diminishing old-time charm. Topped by a new brass-and-iron hood, the range stores cooking pots in the open hearth beneath it.

The graceful high-back stools accented with simple scalloped trim imitate a French design that hints of baronial origin. A custom-made chandelier has the primitive lines of an antique wire-arm candelabra.

With storage at a premium in this small kitchen, the open shelving adds a needed option and interest in the array of country wares on display.

Country Interiors
An Accent
On Antiques

One favorite antique piece, judiciously placed and lovingly used, can add focus to a room. In design, these country kitchens revolve around that single star, though in very different constellations.

In the New England kitchen's dining nook, *left,* a French baker's table—its proportions stout and its wood honey-hued like bread crust—is a visual magnet. Once a pantry, this library-style niche now hosts cozy suppers as the homeowners settle into classic wing chairs.

The small contemporary kitchen, *above,* welcomed the old pine hutch as the solution to a storage dearth. Teamed with the wall-hung cabinet, mellow woods add warmth to the navy-blue-and-white scheme.

161

Blending Old And New

Dual passions—one for blue-and-white china, the other for innovative cooking—guided this kitchen makeover in an 1820s New England home.

The result is an engaging meld in which rich butternut cabinetry, country motifs, and antiques temper slick expanses of stainless steel. Timeworn beams frame a new triple sink below the bay window, and vintage cookware crowns the six-burner commercial range.

On the ceiling, a sprightly print paper sets off the white track lighting, and the pattern repeats in the window's Roman shade. Throughout, the accent color is blue.

A captivating addition is the old file cabinet, *above,* nearly seven feet tall, with more than 100 drawers for kitchen clutter, from everyday thumbtacks to escargot tongs for company.

True to the homeowner's contention that "every room should be personal, interesting, and a bit amusing," one floor tile bears the family dog's paw prints, and the fanciful birdcage holds a collection of blue-and-white china.

Keeping-Room Tradition

Favored since medieval times as a home's hub of activity, the keeping room has evolved into today's combined dining-and-family center, offering the same warmth, comfort, and sustenance it has for centuries. Modern renditions abound, but purists are loyal to spare, rustic spaces anchored by expansive

hearths and furnished with treasured antiques.

In this keeping room in a new Early American-style home, the owners camouflaged the efficiency of today with old-fashioned charm.

For hearthside meals, the family gathers on hoop-back chairs around the old farm-style table, *below, left.* The ample fireplace has room for simmering supper in cast-iron pots. Niches above the mantel appropriately store utensils and pewter tableware, among cherished accents that carry the country mood to every corner.

Old materials and techniques created an efficient kitchen with pioneer reserve, *below, right.* The wainscoting and counter were hewn from salvaged pine. Floor bricks were hand thrown in wooden molds. Wood pegs hold cabinet door stiles. Behind the tall pine cupboard hides the refrigerator. The hanging heirloom fixture was modified to accommodate electric lights.

Country Interiors
A Lofty Retreat

When daydreams turn to getaway places, they may settle upon the humble barn with its spectacular soaring spaces and the cloistered tranquillity of a backroads address.

Often renovated, and sometimes dismantled and moved as this old traveler was from New York farmland to the Connecticut woods, the barn has a character inherently rustic.

Perhaps once a haymow and now furnished monkishly spare, this barn's master bedroom is imbued with surprising elegance and romance, starting with its centerpiece—a 19th-century Scandinavian painted-pine bed, plush in silky linens.

Countering the dark dominance of the crude-hewn pine canopy is a mix of contrasting colors and textures to soothe, smooth, and brighten this attic retreat. The ivory-painted floor offers light and dramatic definition to the center-stage star. Curved pipe-railings add architectural interest. And the nubby woven rug warms with its earthy tones. Newly added windows, beneath the roof's pinnacle, invite the sun. By night, spotlights, nestled in the rafters, take over.

Adding playful spirit and folk art charm to the spare setting is an antique toy, the horse-cycle standing sentry at the foot of the bed.

166

Canopied Tradition

Ancestors slumbered atop straw-stuffed ticks, laid over rope supports, with lumpy bolsters only occasionally softened by feathers. But the colorful beauty of settlement bedrooms compensated for any lack of sleeping comforts.

In a Virginia farmstead, this colonial retreat melds long-ago amenities with today's needs. With its intricate crocheted canopy, the four-poster is a repro-duction roomier than many originals. The imposing carved armoire and colorful bandboxes, *above,* still efficiently store frills and bonnets.

The 1847 Baltimore Album quilt has folk flavor—an American flag and a 'possum atop a log cabin—stitched among its myriad floral motifs.

Framed textiles, a paisley shawl-tablecloth, stenciled chairs and cornices, and a vintage rag rug add eloquent and authentic accents.

169

Duo in Pastel And Primary

Dressing up a four-poster in billowing bed curtains means material gains in style and privacy. In demure gingham, colorful calico, or pristine muslin, such timeless stagecraft still adds a touch of luxury.

Decidedly contemporary fabrics in this simple bedroom, *left*, give a fresh, yet nostalgic, feel with scrubbed-pine pieces and the prim, kit-made bed. On windows and the bed, curtains echo the heirloom quilt's pastel palette. A comfy Boston rocker tempts respite with a good book and a sleepy cat.

Muslin, a staple of the frontier seamstress, is bowed in bed curtains and at the windows of this southwestern bedroom, *above*. The fabric adds soft contrast to the bold, primary-color geometrics of true American textiles—Indian rugs, a chief's blanket, and pieced quilt.

171

Country Interiors
A Quilted Sanctuary

Often country sentiments are expressed best in simple statements. Like precise words picked for a meaningful message, a few well-chosen and well-loved ingredients convey similar eloquence, rhythm, and beauty in a room scheme.

That simplicity is the signature of this peaceful blue-and-white bedroom in a California home, recently redone after a mud slide buried it to the sills. Old treasures were unearthed, cleaned up, and restored, with renewed affection, to places of honor. And this fresh, breezy sanctuary for guests benefited from the loving effort.

Two homeowner favorites—an antique patchwork quilt and an elegant Royal Copenhagen plate displayed in the window—are the tiny room's color inspirations. The minimal furnishings and sparkling-white wall paneling combine to visually enlarge the secluded space.

Accents are primer simple. The eyelet-edged curtains are bedsheets, hemmed along a side and gathered onto a wooden dowel. The quilt's pattern is set off by lace-and-embroidered pillows, making the bed as irresistible to guests as it is to the blue-and-white quilted cat and calico rabbit nestled among the ruffles. A natural vine wreath is a rustic hint of the canyon's deep woods beyond the broad bay window.

173

Four-Poster Favorite

Nestled in a new addition to a vintage-1815 Ohio log cabin, this snug master bedroom reflects a modern-day designer's pride in her pioneer heritage.

Her pursuit of the past began by salvaging the room's old beams and planks from period buildings due for demolition. Her bow to the present is a television discreetly ensconced behind cabinet doors.

Against a backdrop brushed in blue-gray and white, the curly maple four-poster, with a blue-checked coverlet, enjoys the spotlight and a hearth view. In the reading corner, *above,* with its inviting Windsor chair, checks encore in high-tie curtains, a favorite 1820s style.

Artful accents and artifacts—a framed sampler and silhouettes, a bed warmer, and a punched-tin lantern—are the legacy of Midwest homesteaders.

175

Country Interiors
Down-Home Comforts

On frosty nights long ago, warm refuge was often a cozy attic room, the bed piled high with quilts and the wood stove crackling a perfect lullaby. Such scenes are more than memories for the Missouri family at home in a restored, early-1800s log cabin.

Tucked beneath towering rafters, the cabin's bedrooms, sparely set with antique and handcrafted furnishings, have primitive appeal. The pine sleigh bed, *right,* beautifully carved to resemble a dashing, horse-drawn sleigh, is mid-19th century. Vibrant against the backdrop of timeworn woods are the sky-blue patches of the Fence Rail pattern quilt. Prize ribbons, won by the young equestrienne in residence, personalize the room.

The quaint bed, *above,* is a newly crafted version of the old German cupboard bed, an innovation that conserved floor space and provided sleepers privacy and shelter from drafts. Heirloom textiles—a 19th-century New York Beauty pattern quilt and a braided rug—warm the room with color.

Romantic Hideaways

Summoning the sentimental notions of yesterday often produces intimate spaces luxuriously dressed in lace-edged linens and enhanced by inviting ruffles and flourishes.

For this turn-of-the-century bedroom, *below, left,* in a California home that was once a vacation cabin, the homeowners

borrowed from a Victorian forte—romantic style. Yet the era's passion for frills is tempered by refinement. Etched-glass windows remain unadorned, and the sprightly floral wall covering has bold pattern but muted color. Lavish detail is reserved for the fancy iron bed and night table, draped with antique linens in a charming mix-and-match of embroidered and lace trims.

Attuned to an even earlier time, the country haven, *below, right,* has the stenciled charm of the 19th century. Store-bought pillow shams, imprinted with flower-filled baskets, inspired the delicate designs that unify the room scheme. Hand-painted motifs frame the fireplace and border the bed skirt and swag-over-shade window treatment. The sunny, yellow-and-white setting highlights its centerpiece—an 1830s cannonball bed. The patchwork quilt covering the bedside table is a vintage design from West Virginia.

Growing Up With Country

Little girls in couplets may be sugar and spice and all things nice, but aspiring young ladies often fancy more sophisticated country looks over childish clichés. These bedrooms reflect youthful femininity without fussiness.

Garden-fresh patterns in periwinkle blue define the English country bedroom, *left.* Dainty prints in shirred canopy and bed skirt seem to scale down the antique pine bed. Roses bloom on a hand-painted bedside table, and are strewn in buds over the bench seat and trellis-style carpet.

Doubles, from antique beds clad in quilts and crowned with straw hats to dollhouses, are in order in the room, *above,* shared by sisters. Floral wall covering creates a bowerlike air beneath the sloped ceiling.

Accents of nostalgia are the desk chair, reminiscent of an old-fashioned ice-cream parlor, and a wagon bench roomy enough for cherished dolls.

181

Country Interiors
Young Manly Pursuits

Country's rustic simplicity, earthy colors, and robust forms can offer a growing boy lively, livable quarters without turning his private space into a childproof museum.

In a new Ohio home inspired by the designs of the 18th century, this youngster's bedroom takes everyday advantage of aged pieces—a spirited mix of colonial, Queen Anne, and country antiques. Yet it welcomes a boy's playful energy and boundless curiosity.

Handsome bold-checked fabric adds pattern interest to the simple room. Fashioned into canopy and bed curtains, the checks soften primitive angles of the sturdy rope bed.

In tab curtains, the same checks brighten the narrow windows, fitted with "Indian shutters." Hidden inside the wall, the shutters slide out to cover the windows. Once used for protection against unfriendly warriors, they add an authentic reminder of colonial days.

Fresh white walls temper the strong presence of the navy-blue-and-wood tones. Adding definition to the walls around the room's perimeter, the peg rack, a Shaker favorite, is handy for hanging trinkets and clothes and displaying old gameboards.

The history lessons inherent in the antique furnishings are, simply, a bonus for the family's young son.

182

Country Porches And Patios

For shucking peas in the shade, snoozing in the rocker, catching indulgent breezes fragrant with honeysuckle, or just listening to the crickets tune up for their nightly symphony, porches are perfect. Rustic open-air ramblers or new year-round sunspaces, these natural wonders offer room for solitude and socializing. This railed retreat on an 18th-century cabin affords a spectacular view of the meandering Missouri River.

Country Porches and Patios
Welcoming Wicker

As refreshing as homemade lemonade and cool breezes on a sultry summer afternoon, the country porch, decked in wicker, tempts with irresistible comfort and charm.

From the romantic Victorian-style veranda, *left*, in a circa 1890s Florida inn, guests, lazing in rolled-back wicker chairs, watch seaward-bound sailing ships. Dotted fabric cushions add a contemporary accent. In the corner, the fancy-back chair exemplifies the intricacy Victorians favored in wicker.

A quilt collection inspired the cozy reading corner, *above*, in a greenery-filled enclosed porch. Dominant hues from the patchwork palette echo in the dhurrie rug and country-print pillows. When the drowsy feline deigns to relinquish the soft spot, the wicker chair holds the homeowner's reading matter in one cleverly woven arm.

Country Porches and Patios
Shady Invitations

The luxury of whiling away a sunny afternoon on a sprawling porch never changes, but today's accoutrements for lingering go beyond the solitary rocker in the shade. Hot tubs, store-bought awnings, and high-tech furnishings, too, can take to country life.

The railed porch, *right*, complete with redwood hot tub, was added to a 220-year-old cobbler's cottage. This uninhibited mix of Adirondack slat chairs, wrought-iron bench, and wicker rocker provides nostalgic seating. Starched antique linens give inexpensive folding tables a vintage look.

On the latticed porch, *above*, today's sleek carefree furniture assumes a country air. The blue-and-yellow theme of the quilt table cover unifies new and old elements with color. Ruffled pillows in plaid and quilt motifs soften the new chaise longues, resin-coated for weather resistance. A white, sun-shielding awning extends shade beyond the porch roof.

Country Porches and Patios
Of Tables And Twigs

Rambling in railed splendor across the front of the house or secluded in a peaceful niche out back, yesterday's porches extended cordial comfort and rustic charm. The naive and appealing mix of natural seating and handcrafted accents will always say welcome.

Akin to a country tree house blessed with a commanding view of the forest, the screened aerie, *top, right*, fronts a Virginia home perched on a steep cliff. In this transitional space, the wood ceiling and leafy-green painted floor take cues from the outdoors.

The twig settee anchors a nostalgic cluster of collectibles, and, with the wicker table and plant-filled baskets, it enhances an intriguing mix of woven textures. The rag rug, a product of the homeowner's loom, adds a dash of softness and color.

In bygone days, lovingly stitched linens decked out porch tables when company was due. They magically appeared with the bone-china tea service and sterling silver fruit bowl for elegant entertaining.

Though the white table and chairs on the porch, *bottom, right*, are definitely today, the addition of an elegantly embroidered table cover dresses up the setting in turn-of-the-century garden party style.

A century ago, the entrepreneurial handcrafters of twig furniture loaded their rustic wares onto horse-drawn wagons and peddled the seats door to door.

The unpretentious pieces—sculpture with knots, crooked planes, and gracefully bent boughs—have emerged as the perennial favorites for outdoor living spaces. Today, twig pieces are replicated by crafters using age-old techniques.

On the sun-washed deck, *above,* twig furniture adds country flavor and inviting comfort in a somewhat surprising setting—a beach house in Florida redone in vintage style. The gracefully curved seating contrasts with the exterior's boxy angles and extends the home's country theme outdoors.

191

Country Porches and Patios
Sunny Outlooks

Between blooming places and living spaces, there's a beautiful room for compromise.

Whether it grows from a kit or from a requisite remodeling, today's "green room" recalls the lush and fragrant charm of an old-fashioned fernery or Victorian-era solarium.

Eras mingle with sunshine and flowers on this screened-in porch, *left*, the garden spot of a new Connecticut home built in up-to-date efficiency, but true to Early American design.

Against a backdrop of greenery and sunny yellow walls, the room blends new and old. Brushed in white paint, the wicker is new, but eloquently nostalgic. Contemporary fabrics, in sun and sky hues, add freshness and cushioned comfort to the seating. The antique quilt on the settee echoes the bright, new colors, and the heirloom trunk that serves as coffee table wears dark-green milk paint. Adding to the room's outdoor feel is a woven-straw rug.

Once the province of hothouse plants, greenhouse additions now are annexed for year-round, livable space. A recent embellishment to a century-old, Long Island fisherman's cottage, the garden room, *above*, is the build-it-yourself variety, nestled in a backyard bower. The room's serene white scheme unifies a mix of old wicker rockers, pine chest, sleek chaise longue, and contemporary art.

193

An All-Season Sunspace

Glazing expansive arches transformed the open porch on a 1920s bungalow from a fair-weather space into a gracious sun-catcher, as delightful in January as it is in July.

Beneath a bounty of rustic baskets attached to an old ladder suspended at the ceiling, the unchallenged star of the dining area, *right*, is the long, rough-hewn table. For country-style picnicking throughout the year, mixed-vintage chairs and stools encircle the table.

Soft, sherbet hues wash the walls, define the arch trim, and carry the pastel theme down to the nubby striped rug.

Showcased in one graceful arch, an inviting rocking chair anchors the tranquil niche, *above*. The cottage desk is honey-hued pine. Even on the cloudiest days, the chair's warm quilt and plump pillow, covered in country-fresh floral fabric, invite nesting for a while among the old-time collectibles.

194

Country Blooms

Whether your garden space is measured in meadow-size acres or by the inch, fragrant flowers and herbs are a delightful requisite of true country living. And, if contingents of visiting bees, butterflies, birds, and squirrels agree, consider it nature's bonus.

Herbscapes

Deified by ancients and credited, for centuries, with myriad magical and medicinal powers, fragrant herbs flourish in carefree landscapes.

Cape Cod gardener Connie Sutherland's quest for a low-maintenance yard evolved into the backyard herbery, *left*, with more than 100 varieties. Dianthus and marsh mallow are herbal heirlooms from the gardener's grandmother. The ornamental bee skep, *above*, nestles in purple basil, wild senna, lemon balm, love-in-a-mist, dill, and bee balm. In winter, the greenhouse hosts pots of more tender herbs, such as rosemary.

Herbs prefer sunny sites and well-drained, slightly sandy soil. Mulching—leaf mold and cocoa bean hulls are used in these gardens—discourages weeds. Compost and scant doses of fertilizer give gardens a spring boost.

Low-growing thyme, parsley, and lavender are ideal edgings, even for evergreens and rose gardens. In borders, herbs such as sage, lavender, thyme, mint, and artemisia scent walkways as strollers brush by.

Beyond obvious timesaving and culinary advantages of herbscapes, the harvest can be crafted into aromatic potpourri, dried bouquets, and sachets.

199

A Cottage Garden, Wild-Style

Untamed and brilliant with a profusion of blossoms, the medieval cottage garden was a fragrant tapestry of color.

Unlike formal, well-manicured gardens of the landed gentry, these humble patches celebrated the natural beauty of flowers, planted seemingly at random along the garden path to the cottage door.

Cultivating willful blooms in true medieval style is an old-fashioned art, one that southern California artist Karen Kees has mastered with meticulous planning and care.

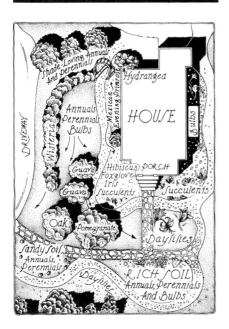

Around her home, *right*, her garden is her canvas. Its semiwild look belies her planting strategies in mixing annuals, perennials, native plants and bulbs for year-round color.

Cottage gardening, she says, imitates art in its use of color and form. Perennials are the mainstay of the never-ending color show, with annuals and bulbs adding variation.

To achieve the informal look, her garden is designed first on paper. The plan, *left*, defines several planting areas. In front of the house, a combination of annuals and perennials—pink, yarrow, salvia, crocosmia, shasta daisy, linaria, and hollyhock—thrives in the mounded bed with rich, well-drained soil.

Special planting areas include a shade border, a daylily bed, a sandy mound for plants sensitive to overwatering, a plot with regular soil and drainage, and a succulents-only dry section.

Just the right magical mix of colors, heights, and varieties may take several years of trial-and-error planting. But, once the growing gets under way, garden maintenance is minimal. Plants native to an area—California poppy, calendula, and ice plant here—make carefree additions to any garden.

A Cottage Garden, Wild-Style

(continued)

Color combinations depend upon where the plants will grow best, look best, and bloom on cue. The variegated border, *above*, mixes the red, yellow, and white of shasta daisy, sweet alyssum, celosia, poppy, calendula, and nasturtium.

A maze of garden pathways, made of carefully fitted flat stones, lures visitors to stroll among the fragrant flowers and allows the gardener easy access for cultivation.

Coreopsis, Queen-Anne's-lace, petunia, salvia, dusty miller, penstemon, and nicotiana create a border bouquet along the walkway, *right*.

If the gardener wants to redesign her blooms, the pathways can be rechanneled by moving their gravel linings.

An automatic drip irrigation system provides each section of the garden with the moisture needed for the diverse plantings to thrive.

The Cutting Garden

The cutting garden, a carefree source for summer blossoms, was once relegated to the backyard zucchini patch. With little tending, old favorites such as zinnias and marigolds reward even the most forgetful gardener with drifts of vivid color.

Whether growing space is measured by the inch in today's small-space yards and gardens or by the country acre, this planting scheme's dependability and vivid versatility make it an appropriate choice. In the Philadelphia home at *left*, a traditional front yard was replaced by a riot of cuttable blooms for formal-style bouquets and informal arrangements, such as the yellow daylilies, zinnias, and sunflowers spilling from an unused fountain, *above*.

205

The Cutting Garden
(continued)

For one-shot bloomers, there is scant room in the cutting garden. The stars are familiar zinnias, sunflowers, marigolds, dahlias, and other flowers that respond to cutting by blooming again and again.

Because the prolific zinnias usually sprout two blossoms for each one picked, these hardy flowers are a colorful mainstay of indoor arrangements, such as the one, *right*, mixed with spiky red bee balm.

Easiest to arrange are single-variety bouquets such as the golden-yellow gloriosa daisies in the iron pot, *below*.

Or mix the cutting garden's harvest in a variety of informal bouquets to add color to gathering spots indoors and outdoors. A bit of freewheeling creativity and baskets full of blossoms are secrets to making lush arrangements. Daisies, lilies, and sunflowers combine with art in a still-life setting, *top, left.* A pretty bowl brimming with the garden's bounty adds fragrant charm to the porch, *bottom, left.*

Even if space is limited, a well-planned cutting garden should provide flowers in abundance. Base the garden scheme on perennials that bloom simultaneously and complement each other in height and color. Add long-blooming annuals for variation. Then, for easy cutting, plant the flowers according to mature size—low-growing plants at the front, medium-size in the middle, and taller ones at the back.

Tall varieties include bee balm, cosmos, dahlias, daylilies, bachelor's-buttons, gloriosa daisies, larkspur, and some marigolds and zinnias.

For midsize color, plan garden space for cockscomb, blue sage, canterbury-bells, some types of bachelor's-buttons, dahlias, and zinnias.

Low-growers include zinnias, marigolds, and prairie gentian. Cushion chrysanthemums, dwarf iris, pinks, and Silver Mound artemisia make pretty garden edgings.

Pick flowers early in the morning when stems and leaves are turgid with stored water. Carry along a container of warm water (100 to 110 degrees Fahrenheit) and immerse the cut stems as you pick. Recut stem ends before they go into the vase, and remove leaves below the waterline.

Country Blooms
Wildlife Temptations

Nature's everyday comedies and dramas open on any backyard stage when furred and feathered actors are lured into the spotlight.

Enjoying the scarlet flash of cardinals or the amusing antics of busy squirrels requires supplying basics—food, water, and shelter. Then, the word seems to spread and a repertory company of wildlife arrives. The Boston backyard oasis, *right*, earned homeowners Betsy and Curt Priest season tickets and front-row seats.

They planted sheltering trees, shrubs, and flowers that produce fruit, nuts, berries, and seeds. Adding an area's indigenous plants ensures that visiting creatures, such as the tiger swallowtail butterfly on the apple blossom, *bottom, left*, will find their favorite foods. The outdoor tables include a flat tray for mourning doves, munching *above*, and a fountain for visiting hummingbirds, *bottom, right*. Seeds, cracked corn, and fresh fruit are daily fare, with suet, a favorite of woodpeckers and jays, added in the winter.

Refreshment options are birdbaths, a bubbling waterfall made of sunken plastic spillways, and a pretty pond. Water is set out in open areas, near enough to trees and shrubs for quick escape from predators.

Country Blooms
Winter Bloomers

Blossoms of a country spring are never out of season, though the calendar insists it's still winter and the weather prophets say snow. A vivid rainbow of amaryllis, crocus, daffodils, tulips, hyacinths, and paper-white narcissus guarantees spring on demand when the indoor gardener uses the technique of forcing bulbs. About three months before the desired debut of blooms, potted bulbs are plunged into a simulated winter—cold storage in a refrigerator, unheated garage, or basement at temperatures 35 to 50 degrees Fahrenheit, but never below freezing. When stems are about 2 inches tall, pots go into indirect light. Planting bulbs at 10-day intervals extends the floral show to brighten winter-weary spirits.

Amaryllis

Buy a treated bulb ready to flower. Choose one that's firm with a robust root system. Bigger bulbs produce more blooms. Before potting, gently separate and untangle the roots.

Soak the bulb's roots in tepid water for three to four hours before planting. Select a 6-inch pot or planter that allows 2 inches of space between the bulb and the edge.

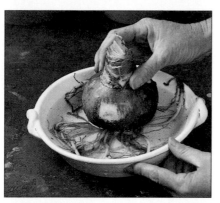

Steady the bulb in the pot and add porous potting soil around it. Leave one-half to two-thirds of the bulb showing above the soil. Moisten, then withhold water until the flower stalk appears.

Set the pot in a sunny window or a room with bright, indirect light and a daytime temperature of at least 70 degrees Fahrenheit. No cold storage is needed to force blooms. Begin normal watering.

Paper-whites

Because the paper-white narcissus grows well in close quarters, 16 bulbs fit in a single 10- to 12-inch pot. Fill the pot three-quarters full with porous potting soil.

Arrange the bulbs in the pot, separating them by about a pencil width. Then gently press them into the soil. A pebble-filled bowl, with water covering bulb bases, also could be used for planting.

Continue adding soil around the base of each bulb until only the necks of the bulbs are visible above the soil. Water well after potting, and maintain evenly moist soil.

Put the pot in cold storage where constant temperatures are above freezing. When bulb stems measure 2 to 3 inches tall, transfer the pot to a bright window that is out of direct sunlight.

211

Coming Home To Country

The quest for the perfect country home, that off-the-beaten-path address with its promise of cloistered tranquillity, leads down roads not usually taken. Perhaps a New England colonial or an old farmstead will win your heart. Maybe it's time to build on tradition—a new house true to centuries-old design. Here are the tales of two country-loving couples who found their dream homes in beautifully different ways.

Coming Home to Country
A Colonial Traveler

For Sam and Becky, their love affair with history began along New England's meandering back roads, where centuries-old homes and treasure-filled shops turn a day in the country into an 18th-century journey.

The venerable colonial architecture held instant enchantment for them. And in the tiny shops, collections of colonial-era antiques waited to furnish the vintage house of their dreams.

Back home in the Midwest, this young couple with a New England-style dream didn't let time or geography stand in their way. They had their 18th-century colonial home, *right,* transplanted to the heartland. It arrived in a 61,000-pound jigsaw puzzle of bricks and beams, all ready for an old-fashioned country house-raising.

The celebrated home delivery culminated long months of waiting and scouting with a

New England man expert in rescuing old homes from demolition. Despite disrepair, authentic homes remain in high demand for restoration.

When they first saw the Connecticut River Valley-style house, *top, left,* that would be theirs, it was simply a house forgotten, partially dismantled and filled with debris. Built in 1755 by Deacon David Sage, it had weathered the American Revolution and more than two centuries with its raised paneling and original buttery, doors, and hardware intact.

As the 10-room house was dismantled, each structural piece—fireplace bricks, stairs, and oak beams—was coded to guide authentic restoration. To guide their reconstruction, the couple compiled measured

drawings, blueprints, and hundreds of slides, detailing every wall and room. Then a train carried it westward, where it was greeted by a crowd of the couple's friends driving trucks and tractors to haul it home.

Before long, the roof beams, *top, center,* rose over the prairie, with the help of a big crane and a crew of hardworking, neighborhood volunteers.

At the back, an addition, *top, right,* provided space for a modern kitchen, baths, and laundry to avoid running water pipes through the old home's beams. A wood-burner was added to augment the four fireplaces original to the old home.

The home is set majestically on the couple's country acres, and its enduring appeal begins at the front door. There, a transom made of reproduction bull's-eye windows recaptures the look of bygone centuries.

214

A Colonial Traveler
(continued)

Though careful to keep the home's historic character, they modified some interior spaces. The "borning" room, where newborns once slept near a warm fireplace, was annexed to the keeping room in the floor plan, *below*. A closet evolved from an understairs chamber, once used to divert smoke for curing meats from the keeping room fireplace.

Set with antiques and colonial accents, the keeping room, *left*, replicates the look of Deacon Sage's day. The massive fireplace, of original bricks, is the focus of this well-used family room. Original brick-red buttermilk paint found on the paneling was matched with new paint. The quilt-draped Windsor chair and wing chair provide soft seating by the hearthside. Accents of pewter plates, crockery, and an old spinning wheel add authenticity to the setting.

With its broad fireplace and paneled walls, the living room, *left*, proved most difficult to restore. Over the centuries, vertical wood panels had been removed from the living room's interior walls to accommodate wallpaper. Old wood, chemically treated with an oxidizing agent to achieve an aged look, was substituted for original wall panels missing.

Against the backdrop of original beams and mellow woods, soft and regal colors, drawn from the oriental rug, unify the mix of furnishings and lend an air of formality. Here, second-hand finds, newly covered, blend with antiques such as the banister-back chair with a rush seat that is circa 1720–1750.

In the dining room, *above*, blue paint on the paneling is a precise match to the original color, a feat achieved by color-coding painted segments as the house was dismantled. The long elegant table is a cherry Hepplewhite circa 1790–1810. The Queen-Anne-style chairs, from the mid- to late 1800s, were purchased in pieces and reassembled. The candle-lighted fixture is a reproduction of a common colonial design.

During the restoration, the couple found traces of their home's perilous past. Around dining room windows there was evidence that large paneled shutters once existed, probably as protection from Indian raids.

Coming Home to Country
A Saltbox Celebration

A clapboard time traveler,
this cozy New England
saltbox puzzles passersby, curi-
ous about its vintage. Its prim
architecture is classic colonial,
the welcoming front-yard tangle
of herbs and flowers recalls centuries-old gardens, and the
weathered picket fence looks
like a hand-hewed relic.

Few would guess that the
charming saltbox, with its mien
of venerability, is new. And
that is just the way Ron and

Lori Lunn planned it. After
months of research and with
loving attention to detail, they
designed a true-to-tradition
country home that marries the
warmth of the past with the
convenience of today.

The couple's goal was "to
build a new house with instant
age," Ron said.

Teamed as home historians,
they drew up detailed plans and
sought out antique materials.
One of numerous museum vis-
its inspired an 1800s design for

the picket fence, embellished
with Williamsburg-type weights
on the garden gates.

Even the abundant gardens,
cultivated in a maze of raised
beds, *above*, were plotted with
precision. New England's historic gardens guided the creation
of the Lunns' gardens, over-
flowing with a mix of sweet-
scented annuals and perennials
and a harvest of herbs for dry-
ing and potpourri crafts.

A Saltbox Celebration

(continued)

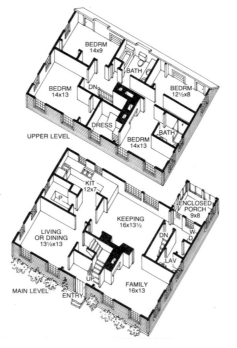

Though more spacious than original saltboxes, the home's plan, *right*, includes a traditional keeping room. Stenciling trims the windows and, with the timeworn appeal of shiplapped pine flooring, sets a primitive stage for the early pine hutch table. Old ladder-back chairs wear original paint. The dry sink doubles as a buffet, and the windowsills display country collectibles.

The 18th-century atmosphere in the living room, *right*, starts at the paneled chimney breast, one of many old architectural elements in the house. Hidden inside the pie safe is the family television. The reproduction sofa and wing chair were chosen for comfort. The tab curtains and lampshade were stitched to match from colonial print fabric.

BEDRM
14x9

BATH

BEDRM
14x13

DN

BEDRM
12½x8

DRESS

UPPER LEVEL

BATH

BEDRM
14x13

KIT
12x7

ENCLOSED
PORCH
9x8

KEEPING
16x13½

LIVING
OR DINING
13½x13

DN

W
D

LAV

UP

FAMILY
16x13

MAIN LEVEL

ENTRY

A Saltbox Celebration

(continued)

In style, the Lunns' country kitchen, *left*, is inspired by Shaker simplicity. But it serves the adjacent keeping room with contemporary efficiency.

Joined by a pass-through, the two spaces are united in color and architectural accent. Soft mustard-color paint, used in the keeping room, is repeated on the plain cabinets. And the peg rack that holds utensils and herbs in the kitchen extends into the keeping room, where it is used to display hang-up collectibles. The reproduction tin chandelier in the kitchen is a twin to the fixture in the keeping room.

The Lunns took advantage of the sloping back roofline of the saltbox to outfit second-floor rooms with amenities. In under-the-eaves bedrooms, such as their daughter's room, *right*, new skylights were installed. The added sunshine and pale color scheme brighten and visually expand the small space. At the roofline's lowest point, the space was enclosed for extra storage. The Shaker-style peg rack, seen throughout the house, adds display space when the old trunk-turned-toy-chest, at the foot of the bed, overflows with treasures.

Dateline: Country

Along America's byways, hidden treasures— historic villages centuries old—perch on the banks of great rivers and nestle beside backwoods roads. Freeways rush past them, and cartographers note them on big maps with the tiniest of dots. Yet, these architectural heirlooms have captured the hearts and imaginations of some special people, those who savor the serenity of country life and are determined to restore and preserve their historic homes. They invite you to step back in time.

Dateline: Country
Mississippi Memories

A century ago, riverboats and ice cream were rites of summer in tiny Elsah, nestled on the Illinois bank of the Mississippi River.

This peaceable, picket-fenced kingdom always celebrated simple pleasures—good neighbors, Josephine Keller's renowned confections, a glimpse of great vessels arriving at Jersey Landing, and the ever-changing beauty of the river road, burnished in autumn and strewn with wildflowers in spring.

Progress flirted with Elsah, settled in 1853 about 30 miles north of St. Louis. But progress took a detour, and with it went the trains, shipping, and mills. Charming Elsah remains firmly rooted in 1800s midwestern America, its historic integrity intact and its vintage architecture now a national keepsake.

Among its more-recent settlers are Mary Ann and Mike Pitchford, who restored the village's 1859 Greek Revival parsonage, *above*. Once used for Sunday worship, the living room, *left*, recaptures the past in simple but elegant country style. A New England slant-lid desk, in old red and blue paint, inspired the colors that showcase an amiable mix of antiques and reproductions such as the handcrafted Windsor chairs.

229

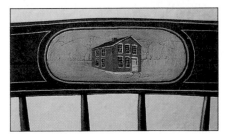

An Oriental rug and spirited fabrics on the camelback sofa and wing chair bring the red-white-and-blue theme to the comfortable seating area. A cherry step-back cupboard displays country wares within. Atop the cupboard, the 1830s Grand Banks schooner has brass fittings and linen sails.

Elsah's heritage is duly celebrated in the Pitchfords' cozy dining room, *left.* The antique Windsor chairs, adding gracious seating around the scrubbed-top table, are embellished with paintings, *above,* of the village's historic homes. The dining room's furnishings and accents are a testament to pioneer craftsmanship. The great pine cupboard, circa 1840, has the bold lines and large cornice typifying German influence. The salt-glazed crockery on top was produced in early potteries around Elsah.

231

Mississippi Memories
(continued)

Proximity to the city and
nearby Principia College has
added writers, painters, engi-
neers, and executives to the village population. Though it is a
daily commute to work in St.
Louis, Les and Patti Sontag so
appreciate Elsah's old-time
country ways and scenic beauty
that they restored the vintage-
1856 stone home, *above,* built by
an early cooper. Typical of the
other pioneer families in Elsah,
the cooper's descendants still
live in the village.

In the Sontags' dining room,
right, Victorian-style wall covering and a companion fabric, in
tab curtains at the windows, set
a tone of gracious formality.
Queen Anne chairs encircle the
round oak table, embellished
with carved motifs around the
rim. Appropriate in this nostalgic setting, the painted-glass
hanging lamp still burns oil.

The basket at the table center
is one of many throughout the
home that the Sontags have
crafted in Ozark style using
white oak splints.

Dateline: Country
A Mill Town Restored

I t seemed the rare chance that country lovers covet. Deep in an enchanted forest, six stone cottages, from the 18th and the early 19th centuries, were for sale at old Hatfield Mill.

Buying the lot and devoting seven years to restoration was not on Jack and Joanne Conti's agenda that day, in the mid-1970s, as they headed for the grist mill site in Pennsylvania's Hibernia State Park. But charmed by the glen's beauty and challenged by the vision of what the dilapidated cottages could become, the Contis bought not one, but all of them.

For their 1810 cottage, *left,* the Contis used 18th-century building techniques and designs such as the stenciling, *above,* copied from a log house nearby.

235

For family-size living space, a circa-1730 log house was joined to the tiny cottage by a compatible central addition.

With its sparse but rich furnishings, the Contis' living room, *left,* summons the convivial spirit of early tavern rooms. The wide-plank floor and ceiling beams were replicated in the same red hue as the original woodwork, destroyed in a fire.

Antique Windsor chairs take advantage of the wide hearth's warmth and beauty. On the mantel and within the old stone fireplace, period accents in iron and pewter find fitting display. The Chinese Chippendale-style sofa is a touch of formality.

In the new center addition, the dining room, *above,* exudes the same sense of history found in the home's vintage sections. Stenciling, in authentic period design, colorfully defines the chair rail, windows, and ceiling line, softening the room's starkness. A 19th-century cherry cupboard displays Adams Company "Palestine" blue-and-white ware. The sconces and chandelier are reproductions.

A Mill Town Restored

(continued)

The salvation of the cottages proceeded slowly as the Contis and their crew became experts in centuries-old building techniques. The stone dwelling, *top, right,* once dormitory space for workers when the settlement's grist mill, iron forge, and general store flourished, remains the most unusual reclamation.

Except for repointed stone walls, a new porch, and painted trim, the exterior of the house today is virtually unchanged. But inside, the original duplex floor plan was carefully renovated into roomy living space for a single family.

New owners John and Dianne Bowders have imprinted their own country style on this architectural treasure, with striking corner fireplaces opening off a central chimney. In their cheery kitchen, *opposite,* the beautiful ceiling beams, mantel, and woodwork, brushed in blue-gray paint, stand out against the whitewashed walls. The chairs' blue-checked fabric and a star-motif quilt on the table imbue the modern furniture with homespun appeal.

In the living room, *bottom, right,* stone walls were again whitewashed to brighten the space and highlight the deep-red beams and woodwork. A wood stove was tucked into the old fireplace for added energy efficiency. Simple down-home favorites—gracious rocking chairs, a soft braided rug, and aged pottery—create an appropriate mood of rustic comfort.

238

Keeping French Traditions

Among the oldest permanent settlements on the Mississippi River's western banks, the picturesque Missouri hamlet of Ste. Genevieve recounts history with a French accent.

For well over two centuries, an indomitable will to survive has helped the village weather perils posed by nature and man. Today, that spirit lives on in Ste. Genevieve's determination to preserve its rich French colonial heritage.

A journey to Ste. Genevieve, about 65 miles downstream from St. Louis, turns time back to the days of explorers, fur traders, and pioneers, when France still controlled most of eastern North America. Visitors stroll among lush gardens, *bottom, right,* some cultivated throughout two centuries.

They linger on the porches where French traders gathered in the 1700s, such as this stone expanse, *below,* displaying cherries picked from the area's bountiful orchards. Testament to the village's French past, the restored cemetery is an irresistible stop for history buffs. Among the headstones is the marker, *opposite,* that reads "Jean Ferdinand Rozier, born in France Nov. 9, 1777 . . . ." Most enchanting is the village's architectural legacy—dozens of 18th-century buildings, such as the circa-1799 Jean Marie Papin house, *opposite, top, right.*

In the early 1700s, rich veins of lead lured hardy French miners to the Ste. Genevieve area. Rule over the growing settlement shifted between France and Spain in the 1760s, before it was claimed by the United States in the Louisiana Purchase. After the great river flooded in 1785, submerging Ste. Genevieve to the rooftops, settlers rebuilt upstream on higher ground.

Longtime residents and relative newcomers such as Linda Vollmar, who owns the Jean Marie Papin house, share the preservation spirit.

Keeping French Traditions

(continued)

Long enchanted by historic Ste. Genevieve, Linda moved from St. Louis a decade ago to the tiny Papin house—three original rooms plus a large loft added in the 1800s. Typical of early settlement architecture, the house is built of vertical log posts, set on a stone foundation.

Linda's love of country furnishings and timeless crafts is reflected in her studio and "wool room," *below,* replete with the necessities for creating the hand-knitted sweaters that have earned her design honors. Aged willow baskets store naturally dyed wool and yarns.

The wool is destined for the maple yarn winder, one of the room's functional antiques that share Missouri roots. The pegged pie safe, made of pine with punched-tin panels, once stood in another historic home in the village. Atop the pie safe is an old pine trough used for butchering. On the wall, the quilt, appliquéd in red and white cotton, is circa 1880–1890 from Perry County, Missouri.

Collectibles here are as varied as the interests of the collector, who is a glider pilot, botanist, watercolor artist, history buff, and outdoorswoman with an enduring fascination with the Indian cultures. A painted Victorian buffet, *top, right,* in a corner of the living room, anchors a sampling of her treasures.

The collection of dolls, silhouetted against the white buffet, include kachina dolls from America's Southwest and a Crow Indian doll that Linda made. On the wall, the infant's portrait is a primitive rendering in charcoal. Seemingly disparate accents—a horsehair pillow topped by a Victorian doily and a beaver pelt reminiscent of Daniel Boone days—soften the old twig rocker.

In the bedroom, *bottom, right,* the star is a maple rope bed, circa mid-1800s, made up in homespun style with feather mattress and flour-sack pillowcases. Peeking from beneath it is a trundle rope-bed that conveniently stows away by day, but extends sleeping space for overnight guests. A hooked rug and a sheepskin warm the wide planks underfoot, and a tufted star quilt adds bold color to the cozy room. Accents are old-fashioned finds such as the German picture, stitchery on paper, above the bed.

Regarded as Ste. Genevieve's premier building and one of the nation's most authentic restorations of the French colonial era, the house *above* was constructed by Louis Bolduc, a Canadian-born miner, merchant, and planter. With wide porches, or *galeries,* steeply hipped pavilion roof, and stockade fencing, it exemplifies French Creole-style architecture favored here in the 1700s. Even the gardens, with more than 250 herb varieties, have been replicated.

The vertical-log walls enclose two main rooms, one chamber for sleeping and the larger room, *right*, that served as a hub for family living and dining.

As in Bolduc's day, the furnishings in this cavernous room, with 11-foot ceilings and cottonwood floors, are spare but gracious. A pine stretcher table is flanked by French-Canadian ladder-back chairs in cherry. Above the table, the adjustable fixture holds beeswax candles. The walnut bread cooler, on the wall by the fireplace, and the circa-1790 cradle are French.

Bolduc's famed fiddle, on the chest between the windows, and his guns over the hearth are among Bolduc family treasures that remain in the house, now open as a public museum.

244

A Pioneer Past Preserved

In the early 1800s, dreams of riches lured miners, traders, and steamboaters up the Mississippi River to the tiny January's Point trading post, a fledgling settlement that lead mining soon transformed into the boom town of Galena, Illinois.

Today, the hamlet's historic homes are legacies of fortunes won there over a century ago, architectural jewels to restore and to treasure. Dubbed "the old banking house," the 1820s log cabin disguised in clapboard, *above,* is one of Galena's oldest, renewed by owners Marianne and Gerry Rapoport. Set with New England antiques, their country parlor, *left,* replays the village's gracious past.

S imple yet formal, parlor seating (pages 246–247) is steeped in tradition. The Chippendale sofa is covered in the muted hues of flame-stitch fabric, and the Windsor and wing chairs are antiques. A chestnut fall-front desk, between the tab-curtained windows, is 19th century. The French "prayer" clock that dates to the early 1800s and circa-1849 coverlet over the wing chair are signed by their respective makers.

As Galena made Civil War history by sending nine generals, including Ulysses S. Grant, to the Union cause, the cabin won its place in local lore. It briefly served as the bank after fire destroyed the offices. Mystery shrouds the home's stone vault. Was it just a fruit cellar or a cache for bank money?

In the cabin's original section, the dining room, *left,* with massive beams and exposed log walls, looks much as it must have long ago. Beneath an old wire-arm chandelier, butterfly Windsor chairs are gathered around the old two-board table for hearthside meals. A fanciful wooden horse and Amish quilt embellish the simple mantel. For requisite silverware and linens, an antique spice chest provides storage on the wall.

Glimpsed through the door on the right leading into the parlor, a massive cupboard displays the homeowners' cherished collections of Staffordshire and Bennington pottery.

A Pioneer Past
Preserved
(continued)

G alena's mining heyday was in full swing when the original four-room section of the brick home *above* was built in 1846. As the prolific family in residence grew, so did the house to its present 14 rooms.

The home's dining room, *left*, with handcrafted furnishings and cheerful pineapple stenciling, reclaims the welcoming warmth of yesterday. The balloon-back chairs, flanking the old table, reflect a favored style of Galena woodworkers. By the window, collectibles are displayed on the grain-painted blanket chest, circa-1841.

Hearts-and-roses stenciling encircles the master bedroom, *above*. Beneath a lacy canopy, the tulipwood bed enjoys a hearth view. An antique bible table hosts fireside tea. A Norwegian cupboard and Sheraton blanket chest extend storage in the small bedroom.

251

Acknowledgments

Designers and Architects

Our thanks to the following designers, architects, artists, and museums, who generously contributed their creative talents and expertise to *Country Style:*

Cover
 Raymond Waites/Gear, Inc.
 Architect: Martin Senell
Pages 6–7
 Alan Kinkead
Pages 8–17
 Elizabeth Nichols
Pages 18–25
 Designer/Builder:
 John Falkowski
Pages 34–39
 Susan Connelly
Page 52
 Monica Greenberg,
 Irma Hariton, Marston Luce
Page 53
 Phyllis Arena,
 The Quilted Acorn
 Stencil: Adele Bishop, Inc.
Page 54
 Top: Bette Zakarian
 Stencil (top): John Houser
 Bottom, left: Peter Kramer
 Stencil (bottom, left):
 Georgia Walsworth and
 Jane Cooper, Country Fare
Page 55
 Design/Architect: Bloodgood
 Architects
Pages 58–60
 Stencil: John Habercam

Page 61
 Monica Greenberg,
 Irma Hariton, Marston Luce
Page 69
 Gretchen Mann/Cobbles
Pages 72–73
 Photography courtesy of
 The Henry Francis du Pont
 Winterthur Museum,
 Winterthur, Del.
Pages 74–75
 Photography courtesy of
 Hancock Shaker Village Inc.,
 Pittsfield, Mass.
 Swivel Chair: Photography
 courtesy of The Henry
 Francis du Pont Winterthur
 Museum, Winterthur, Del.
Page 85
 Photography courtesy of
 The Nelson-Atkins Museum
 of Art, Kansas City, Mo.
Page 102
 Monica Greenberg,
 Irma Hariton
Pages 104–105
 Monica Greenberg,
 Irma Hariton
Pages 114–115
 Carol Anthony
Page 116
 Monica Greenberg,
 Irma Hariton
Page 117
 Top: Bettye Wagner
 Bottom: Gretchen Mann/
 Cobbles
Page 118
 Gretchen Mann/Cobbles
Pages 122–123
 Diane Charnok
 Architect: Jeffrey Charnok

Pages 124–125
 Monica Greenberg,
 Irma Hariton
Pages 128–129
 Nancy Kalin
Pages 130–131
 Raymond Waites/Gear, Inc.
 Architect: Martin Senell
Pages 132–133
 Gretchen Mann/Cobbles
Pages 134–135
 Michael Council/
 Quilts Americana
Pages 136–137
 Kathy Addiego
Pages 138–139
 Diana Charnok
 Architect: Jeffrey Charnok
Page 144
 Robert E. Dittmer
Page 145
 Doris Ream Lawrence
 and Jeffrey Lawrence,
 Lawrence Interiors, Inc.
Page 146
 Carol Anthony
Page 147
 Gene and Carol Arnould
Page 150
 Norman Sinanian
Page 151
 Bill Yoe & Associates
Pages 152–153
 Raymond and Barbara Buck
Pages 156–157
 Michael Haskins and
 Raymond Waites/Gear, Inc.
Pages 158–159
 Clancy Dupepe
 Architect: Michael Carbine
Page 160
 JoAnn Morency

Field Editors

Our special thanks to the following *Better Homes and Gardens*® Field Editors for their invaluable work on *Country Style*.

Pat Carpenter
Barbara Cathcart
Eileen Alexandra Deymier
Carolyn Fleig
Estelle Guralnick
Sharon Haven
Helen Heitkamp
Cathy Howard
Bonnie Maharam
Ruth Reiter
Pat Schudy
Maxine Schweiker
Mary Anne Thomson
Jessie Walker Associates

Photographers

Our thanks to the following photographers, whose creative talents and technical skills contributed much to this book.

Guy Barnes
Peter Bosch
Ernest Braun
Kim Brun
Langdon Clay
D. Randolph Foulds
Susan Gilmore
Bill Hedrich
Hedrich-Blessing
Thomas Hooper
Hopkins Associates
Wm. Hopkins
Peter Krumhardt
Fred Lyon
Maris/Semel
Karen Marzak
Nick Merrick
Mary E. Nichols
Joseph Standart
William Stites
Tim Street-Porter
Rick Taylor
Al Teufin
John Vaughan
John Vaughan and
  Sanford L. Smith
Richard Vincent
John Waggaman
Jessie Walker Associates

Index